Jesus in the Lotus

Jesus in the Lotus

The Mystical Doorway between Christianity and Yogic Spirituality

RUSSILL PAUL

New World Library
Novato, California

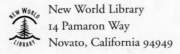

 New World Library
14 Pamaron Way
Novato, California 94949

Text design by Tona Pearce Myers

Library of Congress Cataloging-in-Publication Data
Paul, Russill.
Jesus in the lotus : the mystical doorway between Christianity and yogic spirituality / Russill Paul.
        p.   cm.
Includes bibliographical references.
ISBN 978-1-57731-627-5 (pbk. : alk. paper)
1. Christianity and yoga. I. Title.
BR128.Y63P38 2009
261.2'95436—dc22   2009002430

First printing, April 2009
ISBN 978-1-57731-627-5
Printed in Canada on 100% postconsumer-waste recycled paper

New World Library is a proud member of the Green Press Initiative.

10   9   8   7   6   5   4   3   2

This work is dedicated to a very special trinity in my life:
My mentor, the late Dom Bede Griffiths
My best friend, the late Wayne Teasdale and
My godfather, the late Andre Poirier

Contents

About the Word *God*

FOR THE SAKE OF CONVENIENCE, I have used the male pronoun to refer to ultimate mystery. I am not referring to a particular God, and lesser still a male God, but the notion of an absolute supreme being who is the source of all things, all peoples, and all processes; who is creator, sustainer, and transformer of all existence; and without whom nothing is possible. This great mystery allows for many possibilities, far more than we know of, far more than what we can comprehend, and far more than what we are willing to accept.

Bede Griffiths said that God, ultimate mystery, whatever you want to call it, "cannot be expressed, cannot properly be thought. It is present everywhere, in everything, yet it always escapes our grasp. It is the 'Ground' of all existence, that from which all things come, to which all things return, but which never appears. It is 'within' all things, 'above' all things, 'beyond' all things, but it cannot be identified with anything. Without it nothing could exist, without it nothing can be known, yet it is itself unknown. It is that by

which everything is known, yet which itself remains unknown. It is 'unseen but seeing, unheard but hearing, un-
perceived but perceiving, unknown but knowing.' We speak
of 'God' but this also is only a name for this inexpressible
Mystery."

When I use the word *God* I mean both the personal and
the transpersonal aspects of divinity, all that is revealed in
creation, through symbols and through the mind, as well as
that which lies beyond the scope of our faculties. Although
beyond gender, it embraces both genders and uniquely reveals itself in each as much as it reveals itself uniquely in
inanimate things. All, in their own way, embody and reveal
Divine mystery. Yet we must always keep in mind that the
Divine is always more and that "more" remains mysterious.

Introduction
The Call of the Beloved

EVERY MEMBER OF OUR SPECIES IS INVITED to be a mystic, a seeker of truth, a lover of the ecstatic. We are all called to Spirit. The Divine is always whispering its invitation to us in the innermost space of our hearts. The voice is always there, but it is easily drowned out by the hubbub of our lives. Since you have picked up this book, I assume you are someone who has heard — and really listened to — the Divine call.

Twenty-five years ago I heard the call. In responding to it, I became a bridge between traditions, starting by becoming a Benedictine monk in a monastery that fully expressed itself in the culture of Yoga. I lived and studied under a gurulike figure who was also the abbot of a Christian monastery. Interestingly, my own ancestry is both Hindu and Christian, and through my life as a monk in this Hindu-Christian monastery, I discovered that Yoga and Christianity *can* benefit each other, and that *both* offer the spiritual seeker important insights. This does not mean seekers must convert to another tradition or otherwise compromise the core values of their own. Instead, one can live the best of both authentically and simultaneously. At the very least, one may choose to embrace the parts of another tradition that are most appealing, perhaps even most challenging, in order to evolve and enrich one's own tradition. This is our future: interspirituality.

After almost five years' training as a monk under one of the most important spiritual figures of our time, I chose to leave the monastery, marry, and live as a monk in the world. For the past twenty years, I have published books and music and taught in North American Yoga and spiritual communities, as well as in educational spirituality programs that featured some of the most influential writers and spiritual teachers in the West. My work has continued a dialogue between East and West, Christianity and Yoga, and married and monastic life.

Today, I hear another call, this time to share my journey with others, for the Spirit is calling many to walk this path, one that brings together the best of two very powerful spiritual traditions — Yoga and Christianity — and enables us to heal ourselves and our world. As someone who has traversed the paths of both Yoga and Christianity, and as one in whom these paths have been integrated and balanced, I find myself in an advantageous position, able to share the insights of my journey with you.

Many of us feel a deep loyalty to the traditions in which we grew up. Even after we perceive dysfunction in a tradition, we feel it is still *our* family. If you have felt a call to open up to another tradition, you may be unsure how to respond to the call, or you may have responded in a way that has failed to bring the desired results. Perhaps you are disillusioned with the casualness or faddishness of New Age spirituality. Maybe you are a refugee from mainstream Christianity, frustrated by its focus on externalized rules, practice, right behavior, and salvation without continual inner work. Or perhaps you are too confused or skeptical to have followed any particular path laid down by others. In this book, I offer guidance that springs from my deep conviction that the path to God is paved with many different kinds of stones, some inscribed with profound insights from Christianity and others inscribed with the traditions of the East.

In this book I address a few distinct groups. I reach out to disaffected Christians who feel betrayed by and disillusioned with their tradition, many of whom are ignorant of Yoga. I also address Western Yoga practitioners, many of whom are ignorant of, or indifferent to, or even hostile to, Christianity. There are also millions of satisfied Christians who are extremely prejudiced about Yoga and Hinduism, and I hope this work will help some of them cultivate an appreciation and tolerance for a great spiritual tradition and methodology. These good people, who are passionately following their faith, will find that their faith can both grow and embrace the fullness of Divine mystery by opening to the East in a manner that does not compromise the best parts of the Christian tradition. Many practitioners of the Yogic and Hindu traditions, in turn, harbor an understandable distrust of and prejudice against Christians and Christianity, and I hope these strong views will give way to a better appreciation of what is worthy in Christianity.

A fourth group that I address is one composed of those who feel a strong call to live within an authentic blend of traditions. These new, world souls may benefit most of all

from this work, for a new model of spirituality is crystalliz-
ing today, interspirituality. Arising from a sense that there is
a lack of completeness within the established traditions, interspirituality embraces individuals who seek to live more
than one tradition, authentically and simultaneously.

Please note that I am not talking about syncretism here,
which is based on the idea that all traditions are the same,
and that it does not matter which one you choose. My mentor, Bede Griffiths, spoke strongly against syncretism, as do
I. Syncretism blurs the differences between, and dishonors
the uniqueness of, traditions, and therefore it impairs the
unique challenges for growth that the emphasis of each tradition offers us. Followers of any given tradition can always
point and say, oh, but we too have *that* aspect! But the important question is, how much is it emphasized, and, if it's
emphasized, how effective is that emphasis — how is it
affecting the world today? This brings up the subjects of
form and expression. Christianity, we know, is in crisis; and
form and expression are crucial to that crisis. This is where
Yoga can help, and it can do so by contributing to Christianity without taking away from it.

Christianity in Crisis

A study by the Pew Forum on Religion and Public Life released in February 2008 found that more than one-quarter
of American adults (28 percent) have left the faith in which
they were raised as children. Some have become affiliated
with other religions, while others have left religious institutions altogether. The Roman Catholic Church has lost more
members than any other faith tradition. Nearly one in three
adults in the United States was raised Catholic, but fewer
than one in four is Catholic today. This net loss has occurred

despite an influx of mostly Catholic immigrants from Latin America. Many Americans have adopted Eastern religions. In the United States, where Buddhists make up less than 1 percent of the population, nearly three out of four Buddhists are converts.

In the past two to three decades, large numbers of Christians have turned to the East for spiritual fulfillment, many of them embracing the practice of Yoga. Those who have crossed over to the East have had to let go of their connection to Christianity, for their mother tradition sees their interest in Yoga as a form of betrayal, a straying from their faith. Even if these Christian practitioners desire to maintain some form of connection with their church, there is no real form of support for those who choose to practice Yoga, for churches have no real understanding of it. Invariably, there is a prevailing prejudice and fear among church leaders that Yoga is sinful or anti-Christian, or that it requires one to compromise core Christian beliefs. Some individuals who practice Yoga have been ostracized by their communities, others feel a sense of betrayal, and quite a few keep their Yoga lives hidden. These are sincere human beings who care about the world and take their spiritual development seriously, and such talented and intelligent people, all of them longing for truth, love, and holiness, should not have to feel this way. Given a Christianity that is inclusive and that allows its adherents to practice Yoga too, none of these practitioners would choose to disassociate from their mother tradition. Why does Christianity reject them for using a spiritual practice that can actually deepen their connection to God, other human beings, and creation as a whole?

Folks are leaving the church in droves as they seek to

recover a sense of mystery in their spiritual lives. Ultimately, they are looking for an experience of the mystery of Christ, which has diminished greatly in Christianity because of its excessive focus on the Divine mystery of the human Jesus. This Jesus, supremely divine in an exclusive way, is simultaneously portrayed as an ordinary human. The complex task of portraying him as fully human and fully divine often pushes descriptions of Jesus into contradictory and divergent language, using inclusive yet overly familiar human terms on the one hand together with supremely spiritual yet exclusive terms on the other. This has unfortunately resulted in the gradual decline of the cosmic dimension of religious experience within Christianity that is crucial to an individual's spiritual nourishment and spiritual wholeness, especially in the modern world. Matthew Fox describes this as our loss of *context*, the sense of wholeness derived from being in healthy relationship with the cosmos, that has resulted from the modern preoccupation with *text*, the sense of particularities that stems from anthropocentricism.[1] However, Eastern Christianity, which developed in the first few centuries following the death of Jesus, as well as the Western creation-centered mystics of medieval Europe (Meister Eckhart, Mechtild of Magdeburg, and Julian of Norwich) and ancient Celtic Christianity, offer a cosmic dimension to religious experience, a sense of the vast mystery. This type of Christianity is predominantly wisdom based rather than salvation focused, and it is this type of Christianity that must be revisited if modern Christianity is to recover its depth and relate meaningfully to the Eastern wisdom-based traditions such as Yoga. The sense of mystery found in such traditions appears, in modern Christianity, to have been supplanted by what I call "the domestication of God," which I deal with in the first chapter.

As I travel to Yoga centers and share my work with American Yoga practitioners, I am often struck with how anti-Christian many of them are. Not that they have anything against Jesus. "He's a great guy," I am told. Their problem is with Christianity itself. But what Christianity are they speaking about? Essentially, the Christianity that states salvation is possible only through Jesus Christ. Additionally, one yoga teacher remarked, "I hate being told that Jesus died for my sins, that I am fundamentally bad." She is, or was, Catholic; and her remark refers to a nonhuman or superhuman Jesus. (The lowercase "yoga" refers to any sect, movement, or discipline within the greater tradition of [capitalized] "Yoga.")

What is fascinating is that American Yogis chant to every possible Hindu deity representing every possible facet of the Divine. They are all, as understood in Hindu and Yogic theology, expressions of the One. However, when one offers a chant to the divine Jesus, everyone freezes! He really has no place in their deity world. He's just . . . well, "a great guy!"

How did we get here? Is there really nothing appreciable that Christianity can offer the Yoga community? How about the Hindu community at large? There are over a billion Hindus in the world, and only a very small number of them have any real appreciation for Christianity. Why this small number among such a spiritually sensitive people? In India, where I grew up, there is still a lot of anti-Christian sentiment. In the all-Hindu school I attended in childhood, I knew only one other Christian boy, and I always felt ashamed of my Christian name. Christians, in the opinion of the other students, ate meat, drank alcohol, and engaged in promiscuous sexual behavior while, at the same time, believing that every Hindu was damned and destined for hell. I could feel the heat of their prejudice whenever I had to state my name.

Similarly, here in the United States, I often find myself reticent to state that I have any Christian affiliation, especially among Yoga practitioners. However, as in India, my name is a dead giveaway. Someone recently said to me, "I have your CDs and always thought you were a gray-haired American who lived in India." It is perhaps unusual that I have chosen to maintain my Christian name in a subculture where so many Westerners have Indian names, especially those who are published in the Yoga field. I often joke that "all the good-looking white boys claimed the best Indian names, and I was left only with, well, possibilities such as Häagen-Dazs." Of course, I do have an Indian name, one given to me by Bede Griffiths, who was very much like a guru to me;[2] however, I don't use it publicly. It feels more powerful as a secret, and in this way I get to truly live up to my name without anyone knowing about it.

Before we look at the challenges and benefits that Hinduism and Yoga offer both Christian and non-Christian practitioners, it is important to establish that Yoga is far more than the practice of therapeutic postures that most Westerners associate with the term. Yoga is an expansive discipline with profound philosophical reasoning that embraces the broad scope of human experience. At its core, it addresses the most fundamental need of the human being: to know one's spiritual self and to live in harmony with Spirit, in its absolute form (as spirit) as well as in creation. Does this not remind you of Jesus's injunction "Love the Lord your God with all your heart and soul and love your neighbor as yourself" (Mark 12:30–31)? Yoga, in many ways, helps us understand more deeply what Jesus meant by "self." We explore this in chapter 5.

The Appeal of Yoga

Yoga, in its entirety, represents the best of the East and is perhaps Christianity's greatest spiritual challenge today. Islam, which is Christianity's greatest political challenge, is the second-largest religious tradition in the world, and Hinduism, from which Yoga is derived, is the third largest, with close to one billion practitioners.[3] Hindu spirituality — complex, multifaceted, and laden with many layers of interpretation — is best exemplified in Yoga. Some may argue that Yoga is not Hinduism, that it is universal in its application and therefore not a religion. While this is true, we must keep in mind that Yoga came out of the womb of Hinduism. Additionally, Yoga, which developed in the fire of Hindu spirituality, was shaped by its philosophies and is ensconced in the Hindu way of life. In fact, Yoga can claim universality only because Hinduism in its essence is a truly universal tradition.

Many Christians are discomfited by Yoga and are worried about any relationship that develops between it and Christianity. These Christians accuse the Hindu tradition of converting Christians to nonreligious yoga. While it is true that, in its integration into Western culture, Yoga stripped itself of all religious and cultural associations with Hinduism in order to gain credibility in Western society, the motive was never to convert others to Hinduism or to wean them away from their Christian faith. It is also important to bear in mind that Yoga, as a tradition within Hinduism, historically rejected many institutional and superficial aspects of its own mother tradition. Many of these rejected aspects are the same issues that

Christians have objected to: the caste system, external religious observances devoid of inner understanding, superstitions, and meaningless rituals, to name a few. (There are, however, many meaningful rituals in Hinduism, and only a portion of the tradition can be labeled as superstition. Most of the symbolism is deep and archetypal.)

Yoga is the fastest-growing spiritual phenomenon in the United States and internationally, and many celebrities have embraced its powerful techniques. Christians have to come to terms with the fact that Yoga is here to stay, and that the influence of Yoga is destined to have long-lasting and far-reaching consequences for the development of consciousness in the West and, in all likelihood, the world at large. Even Indians are rediscovering the depth and implications of Yoga and all that it stands for.

Would it not be wonderful if practitioners of Yoga could connect to what is deep and good and powerful in Christianity, in a way that complements the deepest aspects of Yoga practice? And wouldn't it be equally wonderful for Christians to embrace the fullness of Yoga practice without feeling they are betraying their faith and tradition? The sooner we can heal this divide, the better for our world. It will be a great day when the spiritual leaders of the world can join hands and proclaim that a saved Christian, an enlightened Buddhist, and a Self-realized Hindu are equally good, and that a deluded Hindu and a Christian who has not awakened to the core of Jesus's message are equally lost. When we travel across this gorgeous planet, we can see that in all traditions there are both people of integrity and ignorant people: human nature is the same throughout the world, and there are spiritually awakened beings in every race and culture.

The Model of a Yogic Christianity

My hope is that my own journey as an interspiritual seeker, what I think of as a Christian Yogi and World Soul, serves as a template for the future. Again, I am referring not to syncretism but to the simultaneous practice of more than one spiritual tradition, in which the individual is true to both traditions while being honest about the limitations of each. This is an interspiritual model rather than an inter-faith model.

What I am proposing is analogous to the trilevel dialogue that emerged in the Parliament of World Religions, an institution revived in 1993, a century after its first meeting, at which Swami Vivekananda gave the famous speech that many claim resulted in the widespread popularity of Yoga in Western culture today. The idea is that we learn to relate to other spiritual traditions not only with our heads but also with our hearts and our hands. In other words, we engage intellectually, spiritually, and practically — that is, by communally working toward a higher good for all. In this manner, we allow ourselves to deepen, expand, and unite, and to acknowledge both our similarities and our differences.

As Christians exploring Yoga, we must study specific and meaningful ways in which the union of Christianity and Yoga can be modeled in our own lives and spiritual practice. For instance, when Christians explore Yoga together with the sublime philosophy of the Upanishads, they add value and another dimension to their spiritual lives. Their effort does not take them away from the essential substance of their faith, as many Christian leaders fear must happen. There are numerous figures in contemporary times, myself included, who bear witness to such integrity. Aside from Bede Griffiths, there is also Wayne Teasdale, a Christian monk who deeply explored Indian spirituality as a Christian Sannyasi. Teasdale, in fact, coined the term *interspiritual.*

Swami Chidananda, a great spiritual teacher who directs the Swami Sivananda Ashram in the Himalayas, says, "Yoga restores to people, whatever religion they may belong to, the inner spiritual content of their religion."[4] He refers to the mystical core of all spiritual traditions, the inner spiritual life that is the center of any real religion, and without which any religious endeavor becomes merely a facade. When a spiritual seeker is awakened to the mystical life, and he or she becomes truly devoted to his or her own tradition, why should it matter which system served as the catalyst?

We can see therefore that Yoga and Christianity, most certainly the mystical dimension of Christianity, are about the same process: the pursuit of oneness with the Divine. Relating one tradition to the other can be powerful for the world, since each balances and complements the other. At the heart of each tradition is a dynamic and transformative power that, without question, comes from the highest spiritual force in the universe.

The Interspiritual Journey

As I have discovered in my own life, and as exemplified in the life of my mentor, Bede Griffiths, the exploration and integration of Yoga and Indian philosophy need not threaten, or take away from, fundamental Christian beliefs but can add a dimension to them and deepen one's faith. To give you an idea of what interspirituality is like, let me offer a short summary of my initial journey and that of my mentor. Perhaps you will see in it some similarities to your own life or to that of someone you know well.

I was born Roman Catholic in South India. Although my family was Catholic, all I knew of Christianity was its clerical institutions — hospitals, schools, parishes, and charities. I was fascinated with Hinduism, a tradition I did not truly understand or properly express, even though my maternal ancestry has Hindu roots and I was surrounded constantly by its vibrant spiritual culture. My parents, like most Indian Christians, lacked real knowledge of Hinduism and were often suspicious and at times fearful of it. My attraction to Hinduism remained undeveloped until, in 1984, at the tender age of nineteen, in a dramatic act of formally renouncing the world, I went to live under the direction of the renowned spiritual maverick Bede Griffiths.

While living as a Benedictine monk under his guidance, I studied Yoga, mysticism, Sanskrit chanting, and Indian classical music with many wonderful teachers, since he encouraged the development of a wide range of knowledge and spiritual skills and practices. This book explores the Eastern practices I have used to deepen my spiritual journey as a Christian monk, particularly Yoga, and the remarkable mystical experiences I had as a Benedictine monk and Yogi. Throughout my spiritual life, I have tried to heal the sort of tensions between Eastern spirituality and Christianity that I have encountered since childhood, tensions that I see as being prominent in the United States and in the West as a whole today. Sadly, Hindu-Christian tensions that continue in India seem to have escalated in some parts, especially during the past few years as I wrote this book, resulting in dozens of deaths, the burning of homes and churches, and even the rape of a nun.[5]

In Bede Griffiths, I found the perfect combination of a Christian mystic and Hindu holy man. Born an English

Anglican, he was educated at Oxford under the tutelage of
the literary genius C. S. Lewis, who became his close friend.
Bede started out as an agnostic. An experiment in studying
the Bible as literature led him to Catholicism and eventually to Benedictine monasticism. For almost twenty-five
years, he lived the quiet and hidden life of a Benedictine
monk in an English monastery, until he met Tony Suzman,
a disciple of Carl Jung. Under Suzman's influence, Bede's
life took a radical turn, particularly when she introduced
him to Eastern spiritual writings such as the Bhagavad Gita.
This classic Yogic scripture, along with the Upanishads
(Hinduism's New Testament), would influence his Christian faith and experience for the rest of his life.

When Bede felt called to explore India and Indian spirituality, he did so without giving up his Christian faith and
religious commitment to the Benedictine way of life. In
stark contrast to his earlier, English life, he spent the latter
half of his life in the garb of a Hindu mendicant monk,
meditating on the Hindu scriptures and seeking to understand his Christian faith in light of the Yogic experience of
India. His deep reflections, born of many decades of com-
parative study, and coupled with his rich inner spiritual life,
informed my own spiritual development.

The life and work of Bede Griffiths and others are invaluable testaments to the power of Christianity's union
with Yoga. In outlining my own spiritual journey in this
work, I seek to explore the potential of that union even further. There is also an added therapeutic benefit of Yoga that
should interest Christian practitioners: medical science and
innumerable case studies in a variety of disciplines attest to
the tremendous healing power of Yoga.

I sincerely hope that this book will inspire Christians to

understand and embrace some of the powerful methods and teachings of Yogic spirituality and to integrate it into their faith experience. Likewise, I hope that Yoga practitioners find new ways to relate to Christianity without the hardened resistance that is presently characteristic of so many. My book also addresses nontraditional spiritual seekers and young people looking for spiritual insight and may help them understand the value of the mystical journey, which is a universal process.

The Benefits of Interspirituality

What do we stand to gain by relating and combining the worldviews of Christianity and Hinduism? In essence, the former emphasizes relationship, the latter identity. Both are important, and there are individual and collective benefits to relating the two, including the strength of cross-cultural harmony, which can contribute significantly to the peace and stability of our world. While Christianity, with roughly 2.1 billion practitioners,[6] is the world's largest and most powerful religion today, Christians stand in danger of isolating themselves from the rest of the world, in an us-versus-them scenario. This is because of popular Christianity's exclusivist doctrines and strongly extroverted spirituality, which, arguably, have value but are in need of balance. The present tension between the Western world and the Middle East is largely a result of the long-standing tensions between Christianity and Islam, which is just as exclusivist and extroverted (except among mystical sects, most notably the Sufis). The Islamic population is rapidly growing, as is the Hindu population. Tension between Christians and Muslims is so strong that it will take a long time to eliminate it. Furthermore, it is difficult for practitioners of these two religions to collaborate spiritually, since both have exclusivist doctrines fundamental to their faith.

Yoga — like the Hinduism from which it is derived — is broad, deep, universal, inclusive, flexible, and tolerant. A Christianity informed by Yoga's rich inner mysticism and Hinduism's profoundly inclusive worldview can rediscover itself in a new light and inspire a greater proportion of the world's population. This is possible because Yoga and many wonderful aspects of the Hindu spiritual tradition can support rather than threaten Christianity. In fact, the two can complement each other in marvelous ways, as we will discover. The benefits of this union may well extend to Islam, which today, as a result of political conflict, is also rediscovering itself. In this context, great tribute must be offered to the Sufi community, which, for almost a millennium, has sought to integrate the best elements of mystical Hinduism, Yoga, Christianity, and Judaism.

Yoga, which is not a religion in the strict sense of the word, demands to be taken very seriously. It is not only ancient, with a formidable five thousand years of history and development, but also tremendously effective in a wide range of therapeutic applications well recognized by the Western medical community today. Christians, even if grudgingly, have to come to terms with the fact that Yoga is a credible discipline, not just physically and psychologically, but spiritually too. In fact, quite a few Christians practice the physical form of Yoga without recognizing its spiritual roots and philosophies and still derive the deeper benefits naturally built into the system. However, when Christians open themselves to the wisdom of Yoga's deep insights, their faith experience and personal spiritual practice can only be enriched.

Conversely, Christians' embrace of Yoga can just as well invite Yoga practitioners to look more closely and deeply at the core values that Christianity has to offer the East. However, if Christians are to determine Christianity's values and strengths within the context of a global spiritual perspective, and know what it can truly offer the East, they must first understand and appreciate Yoga's spiritual depth and power.

I am not suggesting that Yogis, or Hindus, become Christian any more than I want Christians to become Hindus. The intention behind this work is not about conversion to either path. My hope, rather, is that Christians and Hindus heal the wounds that intolerance, lack of knowledge, and prejudice have generated. Christianity has not been very kind to Hinduism, and the wounds run deep, but they can and must be healed, for healing them will make our world stronger. Additionally, there are Christians deeply committed to their faith who also have an interest in Yoga, whose techniques and mystical insights they are afraid to embrace because they distrust the tradition. This is a conditioned distrust founded on irrational fears and the lack of unprejudiced discovery of the value and spiritual compatibility of Yoga with Christian faith. It is my prayer and hope that this book helps in some way to change it.

However, as we know, all change has to begin with individuals. When I speak of Christianity in this book, I often try to link it strongly with the Jewish tradition in which it was birthed, just as Yoga was birthed in Hinduism. Any individual who allows himself or herself to be influenced by the powerful crosscurrents between the two traditions — Judeo-Christianity and the rich complex of Hinduism and Yoga of which Buddhism, Jainism, and Sikhism are part

— will be pushed to the forefront of evolving consciousness. These cross-cultural prototypes represent the spirituality of the future that is being birthed in our time. Ours may be a personal journey now, but we are being called to forge models for the future, for we are at a cusp period in our history, one that is of momentous significance, as significant as the invention of the wheel, the discovery of fire, the birth of the printing press, or all of these and more put together and magnified many times over. My explanation of how those crosscurrents can enrich the personal spiritual journey of the individual, how the discovery and the opening of this mystical doorway can affect the life of the individual seeker, is perhaps the most powerful message of this book.

I

Christianity's Domestication of God
The Gap between Words and Actions

ARUN GANDHI, the fifth grandson of India's legendary leader, Mohandas K. "Mahatma" Gandhi, and cofounder of the M. K. Gandhi Institute for Nonviolence, tells the following story about his grandfather:

In the mid-1930s when the leader of India's oppressed class, Dr. B. R. Ambedkar, announced that 150 million of his followers who were (and still are) regarded as "untouchables" would convert to a new religion, many Christian and Muslim religious leaders came to India to get a slice of the religious cake. Many stood on street corners of Indian cities denouncing the evils of Hinduism, explaining how the "untouchables" would find equality and dignity if they converted to Christianity. Weeks went by and not many of the "untouchables" took advantage of this offer. One day, Rev. E. Stanley Jones of the United Methodist Church asked my grandfather,

M.K. Gandhi, why the "untouchables" were not
accepting the Christian offer. Grandfather's reply
was "The day you stop talking about how good
your religion is and start living it, everyone will
want to join it."[1]

These are strong words, reportedly uttered by one of the
most influential figures in contemporary history and someone for whom the New Testament, especially the Sermon
on the Mount, was as important as his own scripture, the
Bhagavad Gita. Although a devout Hindu, Gandhi demonstrated to the world what turning the other cheek looked
like in modern-day circumstances. Paradoxically, he turned
the other cheek to Christians who were oppressing him and
his people. And turning the other cheek, as scholars now
inform us, was not necessarily an act of submission in Jesus's
times but quite possibly a brilliant act of loving defiance,
and Gandhi used it rather effectively.[2]

Gandhi's first encounter with Christianity was said to
have taken place when he sought to attend a church service
in South Africa. Deeply moved by his reading of the Bible,
he was seriously considering becoming a Christian. However, a white church elder refused him admittance and
spoke to him in insulting and racially divisive language, in
stark contrast to Jesus's most important directive to "love
your neighbor as yourself." Gandhi apparently vowed at
that point to practice all that was good in Christianity, but
without becoming a Christian affiliated with the church.
(Another often-quoted declaration of Gandhi's: "When all
Christians live by the Sermon on the Mount, I will be the
first to become a Christian."[3]) I experienced a subtler version of racism when attending a service in the United States

recently. Most people ignored me, and many appeared to be uncomfortable when interacting with me as part of the service, particularly during the "greet your neighbor" part. How did we get here? When did Christians, once oppressed for following the teachings of Jesus, become the oppressors?

It is this contradictory expression of Christianity, professing one thing and doing another, that has created a great rift between Christianity and the Hindu tradition. Hinduism, although it has many clear rules and practices of its own, is supremely tolerant of other belief systems. Nonetheless, despite aggressive missionary activity in India since the fifteenth century, and despite a Christian presence in India since the fourth century (or earlier), slightly more than 2 percent[4] of this deeply religious country is Christian. And those who convert to Christianity sever most of their ties to their culture and their extended family for the same reason that most Christians who practice Yoga or another Eastern spirituality in the West must relinquish most of their connections to their birth tradition.

Latin Christianity and evangelical Christianity emphasize salvation through the profession of faith in Jesus Christ as Lord and Savior far more than the essential teachings and spiritual experience of Jesus. Without doubt, this has prevented many Hindus from truly appreciating and accepting the best that Christianity can offer. Additionally, because there is so often a stark contrast between the ideal and the expression, aggressive preaching (especially in India) often falls flat on its face. Gandhi often implied that Christians could preach far more effectively through their actions than through their words. Words, however, have become the cornerstone of Western Christianity, and the language of Christianity is often divisive and unhealthy, having been formulated from a position of superiority and prejudice toward other traditions. In fact, the issue of language in itself has caused many Christians to disassociate with the church.

The purpose of this chapter is not to criticize Christianity but to explain why the West needs Eastern spirituality today, and to identify some of the tensions that prevent such an exchange. Indeed, to criticize Christianity would be to criticize a tradition that is an essential part of my ancestry, one I continue to hold in great esteem. As you continue reading, you will see that I have a deep love for Jesus and that I understand the unique significance of his life, death, and essential message of the Kingdom of God, which I understand in terms of consciousness. Furthermore, I appreciate the many mystical concepts of St. Paul, such as the mystical body of Christ, and I have been awed by the writings of many great Christian mystics, including Meister Eckhart and St. John of the Cross. However, there can be no doubt in any rational person's mind that the West is in need of balance. Could this imbalance relate directly to the imbalance within Western Christianity? Some of the best parts of Eastern spirituality, especially Yoga, can contribute to restoring this balance. The East is not perfect either and can benefit from certain Western values, particularly from those values emphasized by Christianity that have shaped the West in positive ways. These core values must be retrieved, redeveloped, and reestablished.

My mentor, Bede Griffiths, was clear that the restoration of balance in Christianity will come only with the Western recovery of the intuitive mind, a corrective to its excessive rationality. At this time, the tools for such a recovery are readily available from the East, from the other wisdom traditions, which, of course, include Yoga. For this to happen, a meeting must take place at the deepest levels of human consciousness. Bede called this is the marriage of East and West that can be realized in the melding of Christianity and Yoga.

God's Separateness: Excessive Transcendence

Perhaps the problem of imbalance in Western culture, and consequently in Western spirituality, stems from the most fundamental attribute of God as described in the Semitic traditions: God's holiness. Bede put it this way: "In the Semitic tradition, God is represented as the transcendent Lord of creation, infinitely 'holy,' that is, separate from and 'above' nature, and never to be confused with it."[5] Furthermore, God's injunction to Adam, to "be fruitful and multiply; fill the earth and subdue it" (Genesis 1:28), has largely determined the West's relationship with the natural world and its domination of other cultures through colonial rule. The two together have resulted in the great destruction of the earth's natural resources and, in the past, intolerance toward the spiritual inclinations of indigenous cultures. Unlike indigenous cultures, Western peoples have tended not to replenish what they have taken from the earth and have not practiced taking in moderation. This has brought on global warming and other ecological imbalances. Is it not evident that our relationship with our planet is directly associated with the way in which we understand God?[6]

The understanding of an overemphasized transcendence — that is, one not balanced with immanence — has caused Western Christianity to estrange itself from the multiplicity of forms expressed not only in nature but also within the infinite creativity of the human mind, especially in the sacred language of myth and its symbols.[7] This understanding has placed God far away from our world of form and matter, in contrast to, for instance, the beliefs of many tribal cultures that have a strong sense of innate sacredness within nature. The East offers us a sense of the immanence of God, a sense that God is near, and within, us and in the varied forms of existence. Additionally, the East offers us the opportunity to understand and experience the mystery of God in nonanthropocentric terms.

The problem with an excessive focus on transcendence is excessive rationality, which is an abstraction from everyday reality. One way of describing rationality is as thinking that is distanced from feeling and the direct experience of being. Bede pointed out that the Western psyche has its roots in the teachings of Socrates and the Greek philosophers, who developed the analytical mind, one that focuses on making judgments and on concepts. From the time of Jesus to the Renaissance, this type of mind, along with the oriental mythology of the Semitic Christian world, produced a somewhat balanced system that left a record of its tremendous achievements in the art, architecture, and mystical theology of the Middle Ages. However, during the Renaissance, this balance was lost, and the aggressive, analytical mind took precedence in society, as it still does today. It has resulted in the extreme separation of conscious and unconscious, mind and matter, soul and body. Western philosophy, Bede pointed out, swings between the two extremes of materialism and idealism as a result of a disease of the mind, a type of schizophrenia, that has developed since the Renaissance, when the united vision of the Middle Ages was lost.[8]

Excessive rationality is epitomized in the famous statement of René Descartes, "I think, therefore I am." And it is evident from our manic Western lifestyles that the machine (the autonomous thinking mind) has taken over. The East, too, has developed powerful rational, logical, and analytical skills, but these are balanced with a sense of "beingness." This sense of beingness is what we refer to as the mystical dimension, meaning that it is hidden from normal perception as it is concealed by the content of our mind and our identification with the content. The phenomenal success of spiritual teacher Eckhart Tolle has illustrated the great hunger for the mystical dimension felt by so many North Americans and Western Christians. Tolle taps into the spirituality of India, although he uses contemporary language and the model of the human psyche to help bridge the gap between the highest spiritual experiences of Yoga and the experiences of contemporary living. The spiritual experience of Yoga is based on the joy of being, which is markedly different from the "joy of having something," which is touted incessantly by the advertising media. Much angst in the Western psyche stems from the illusion that one has to "have something" in order to be happy. While this same mentality is penetrating the East, especially India, most people there are still happy simply in their sense of being, a fact that is evident to almost everyone who has been to India, even recently. In India, people might be starving or living in abject poverty, but still they have an unmistakable joy in their sense of being that is conspicuously absent in the West. This joy comes from the indigenous spiritual tradition of India. It is this joy that we must rediscover in the West, and Yoga is already proving to be the methodology that can help bring this about.

Disregard for the Earth and the Feminine Face of Divinity

The domination of nature — the "rape of the earth," as it is sometimes called — is also reflected in Christianity's view

of the feminine. There is a maternal quality to the earth that
every indigenous culture around the world has recognized.
Before the shift to patriarchal domination that began roughly
five thousand years ago, many of the early civilizations —
including the Mesopotamian, Egyptian, and Indus Valley
civilizations — were matriarchal. India is perhaps the only
ancient civilization that has continuously honored this matriarchal presence. Christianity has had a hard time accepting the feminine as divine. For instance, even though Mary
is referred to as "the Mother of God," she is not "God" herself but simply a channel for male divinity. The long and
heated debate over women priests in the Catholic Church
implies that women are not spiritual enough for the role. Yet
psychological testing clearly reveals that women are more
spiritual than men. Additionally, the fact that the gender of
attendees at spirituality workshops and retreats is predominantly female, along with women's interest in spiritual matters as evidenced by their purchases of spiritually related
products, demonstrates that women are more active spiritually than men.

The East offers us a balanced view of Divine gender as
well as the transgender aspects of the Divine. Hinduism
and Yoga regard the Divine as being he, she, and it, for the
tradition recognizes that all pronouns are simply a convenient way of communicating with and about the Divine.
However, the mystery of the Divine is infinitely more than
what can be expressed in human speech. Almost every
Hindu recognizes that the image — masculine, feminine,
or abstract — is simply the medium through which an exchange of energy and information takes place. Do we not
use a similar principle in understanding how the communion wafer transmits the mystical consciousness of

Jesus? Yet for hundreds of years, Hindus have been accused of being idolaters.

Additionally, the East offers us powerful models of the sacred feminine as a legitimate face of the Divine, which many in the West crave. This is one of the reasons for the broad appeal of the Hindu symbols and mythology-based artworks that are now conspicuously displayed in yoga studios across the country.

Disregard for the Human Body

When Bede Griffiths first arrived in India, he was mesmerized by the naturalness of people's movements. He wrote, "Whether sitting or standing or walking, there was a grace in all their movements and I felt that I was in the presence of a power of nature."[9]

Christianity is essentially about the body, as exemplified by the crucifixion and the resurrection. However, Christianity in a sense also disregards the body and human sexuality. The great saints of Christianity sought to subjugate the senses; for instance, to suppress their sexual instinct, Saint Francis of Assisi reportedly threw himself naked in the snow and Saint Benedict rolled in thorns. Although such dramatic acts are relatively unknown today, the lack of nutritious food in many Christian monasteries and retreat centers across the United States continues to demonstrate this underlying, if unconscious, dispassion for what is, in Yoga, our most powerful and sacred vessel of Self-realization — our body. Christianity has paid little attention to diet, relying more on the statement by Jesus that what proceeds out of a person, meaning what a person says and does, is more important than what goes into a person (Mark 7:15). There is great wisdom in this teaching, but Jesus said it in a context of ritual cleanliness, not health. Unfortunately it has also prevented Christians from learning how to use and develop their bodies so that they become assets in their spiritual life and growth.

This estrangement from the body goes back to the early Greek philosophers, who distanced themselves from the body through their emphasis on concept. Indian philosophical systems, on the other hand, are rooted in contemplative experience that integrates intuitive vision, refined by tuning the body through the practice of yoga and meditation, and analytical thought, which enables the Indian spiritual tradition to maintain a healthy balance. Most seminarians in Christian spiritual training could benefit greatly from learning how to integrate yoga practice into their spiritual life. This, of course, would, in addition to the philosophy and spiritual practice, also involve learning more about the relationship between food and spiritual experience. Catholic priests, nuns, and monks are required to be celibate but are not shown how they can be celibate in a healthy way. Again, the combination of yoga and diet can offer some powerful tools for the healthy integration of sexual energy.

Even in marriage, which is celebrated as a sacrament in Christianity, the body is often subconsciously equated with "the flesh" (an analogy for "lower nature"). Many Christians, especially Catholics, see human sexuality as simply a practical function, somewhat like defecation, rather than as a spiritual force, and it is rarely spoken of in a spiritual context. For many Catholics, sex is something "dirty" and meant to be kept in the dark, which is extremely unhealthy. The sexual abuse among Catholic priests, along with the hundreds of millions paid out in lawsuit settlements that reflect the deep damage done to so many, is a clear indication that this does not work.[10]

Yoga can help Christians realize that the body is an essential vehicle for spiritual realization, and Yoga can help to integrate the body and its processes more intimately in prayer experience. In contrast to subjugating the body, such as by kneeling on rock salt while praying or by lashing it with a whip, Yoga shows how the body can be loved into prayer.

The Problem of Language

Saint Paul was perhaps the most influential figure in the Christian community during the years following Jesus's death. In order to bolster the religious infrastructure of early Christianity, he borrowed from Greek philosophy and Roman culture, providing a philosophical and theological language for his fellows. This language and culture have dominated Western Christianity and, in a sense, exhausted its possibilities. Now, after two thousand years, Christianity has an opportunity to engage with the East, with the language of Indian philosophy and the culture of Yoga. Imagine the potential! As Paul's namesake, I like to think that he is in some way working through me to bring about this new phase.

When in the mid-1960s the Catholic Church stopped using Latin in masses, this took out all sense of mystery. The awkward familiarity of the vernacular may have, in some respects, made the Divine more accessible, but it simultaneously domesticated the mystery of God in the same way that we domesticated animals and the earth.

The domination of reason and rationality in the Western world since the Age of Enlightenment, coupled with, in the past few centuries, the disappearance of intuition, has led to the loss of the contemplative, or mystical, dimension of Christianity. As a result, Christianity has become predominantly a thinking religion, and many have turned to the East for experiential nourishment. Yoga is satisfying this contemplative need, giving people respite from the incessantly thinking mind and reintroducing them to the sacredness of the body.

Since the Protestant Reformation, some Christians have insisted on a literal interpretation of scripture. The Jesus Seminar, a group of international scholars dedicated to deducing what Jesus really said (and what he did not), seeks to discern where "history has been metaphorized" and where "metaphor has been historicized." Noted Jesus Seminar scholar Marcus Borg explains: "the Bible combines historical memory and metaphorical narrative. Certain factual aspects seem metaphorical. For instance, the exile in Babylon in the sixth century BCE really happened, but the way the story is told gives it more than a historical meaning. It became a metaphorical narrative of exile and return, with abiding images of the human condition and its remedy. The Genesis story of Creation, the Garden of Eden and the expulsion of Adam and Eve ... are what might be called purely metaphorical narratives."[11] Trying to insist that humanity was spawned by an Adam and Eve who are factual and literal and historical figures who lived about 5,000 years ago in the light of overwhelming scientific data that places the presence of humans on our planet hundreds of thousands of years ago is an instance of a metaphor that has been historicized. However, as Borg brilliantly suggests, metaphorical meaning is the more-than-literal meaning of language and should not be assumed to be less valuable than factual meaning. By distinguishing between history and metaphor, and relating the two to each other, we can actually deepen our faith and relate intelligently to tradition.

The emphasis on the Bible as a literal, factual record, which many conservatives promote, often poses serious problems for the scientific-minded person,[12] for whom faith is seen as requiring a compromise of intelligence and rationality. This has resulted in the resurgence of fundamentalism and a chasm between people of faith and people of science. The solution is in the problem: language. Many scientists, as well as people of scientific inclination, are profoundly spiritual people, and today a universal language is developing that can bridge science and spirituality. As the respected scientists Fritjof Capra, Peter Russell, Amit Goswami, and Rupert Sheldrake — all of whom have been deeply influenced by Indian spirituality — have demonstrated, the language of Eastern spirituality has the strength to create such a bridge.

We are perhaps only now coming to terms with the death of God that Friedrich Nietzsche proclaimed in the late 1800s. A much-loved and much-respected Episcopal bishop in the United States, John Selby Spong, writes, "The evidence that God, understood theistically, is dying or is perhaps already dead is overwhelming. I define the theistic God as a being, supernatural in power, dwelling outside this world and invading the world periodically to accomplish the divine will."[13] This is the male deity far removed from the world that we have been discussing, and this definition points to the language that has been built around this deity, such as *Father, God in Heaven*, and the *One True God*.[14] Western Christianity has excessively focused on male, patriarchal language for sacred experience and this, again, has worn thin and lost its power to affect us. As mentioned in the introduction, many Christians and Jews who chant *kirtan* (praising God in both genders and in various manifestations) are extremely uncomfortable about chanting the name of Jesus. The reason: Jesus is male and the son of a male God who is far away and who is a judging entity. Additionally, Jesus too is often presented as a judge. The Catholic Church has slowly added some inclusive language to its liturgy, but it still has a long way to go.

Additionally, many Yogis are disturbed by the militant and negative language of Christianity, by terms such as *the anti-Christ, the devil, eternal punishment, burn in hell,* and so on. This sort of negative language dominates our health system as well. At a conference on integrative medicine hosted by the Inner Connection,[15] I heard a remarkable physician, Dr. Gladys McGarey, point out that Western medicine is overly focused on disease, and that its language is antilife, focused on attacking and destroying: antibiotics, antiaging, anti-inflammatory, and so on. The language of the Bible, especially the Old Testament, is often not much different. The language of Yoga and Eastern mysticism, on the other hand, is pro-life, and this is another reason why it can be so helpful to us today.

Also of note is the fact that the language of Christianity can be psychologically depressing, particularly concerning the guilt presumably attached to our being born in sin. The yoga teacher I mentioned earlier told me, "You know, it's a lot of heavy stuff to be constantly told that we're bad, and that Jesus died for us because we are bad." The excessive emphasis on the suffering of Jesus, his agonizing death on the cross, and his bearing the weight of our individual sins on his shoulders: these are the images that have dominated the spiritual life of Christians, and many today find this emphasis objectionable. Perhaps it had value in the past, but we have to ask ourselves how useful it is to us today. If the church can express its mystery in the language of Yoga, which is the language of consciousness, more Yogis will relate.

From Mythic God to Levels of Consciousness

Our vision of, knowledge of, and relationship with the Divine have evolved over the ages. As Jim Marion eloquently points out, the concept of the mythic tribal God of the Old Testament, who later found new expression in and through the teaching of Jesus, has, sadly, continued to dominate Christian life and teaching. Many people today reject the notion of a mythic tribal God who is partial to a certain racial segment or responds well only to those who believe in his exclusive lordship. And many other Christians who appreciate the new covenant in Jesus still hang on to the old mythic deity that Jesus helped to refine. However, I see movement toward a new paradigm, one that has been outlined by Jim Marion. He interprets the evolutionary prediction of Julian, the abbot of an Italian monastery (1132 to 1202 CE), as saying that we moved from the age of the Father — the three thousand years preceding Jesus — to the age of the Son during the past two thousand years, and have now entered the Age of Spirit (the Aquarian Age), which is also the age of interspirituality.[16]

Its exclusive focus on Greek philosophy and Roman culture gave Western Christianity tunnel vision. As Griffiths has pointed out, "Christianity was originally an Eastern religion (like practically all religions), but its movement has been predominantly westwards. It passed with St. Paul through Asia Minor to Greece and Rome, and then in the course of time to Europe and then America. As a result, though always retaining its Eastern basis, it has become a Western religion, with Greek theology, Roman organization and essentially European culture."[17]

What the West needs most of all from the East is the Eastern understanding of levels of consciousness. Ken Wilbur — the Carl Jung of our times — has written extensively on educating the Western world about the Eastern understanding of consciousness. This understanding is crucial if we are to better understand the spiritual journey and relate the deepest mystical experiences of Jesus to the mystical depth of the Yoga tradition. For instance, Christians need to understand the nondual consciousness of Jesus — "I and the Father are one" — in the light of Yoga, and to discover how to participate in that experience. At present it is regarded as an experience reserved strictly for Jesus, and while much is made of it, little or no attention is paid to the fact that such an experience — oneness with the source of one's being — was known and documented in the Indian tradition five hundred years before Jesus claimed it. It was revolutionary in the Semitic world, but it was regular fare in India. In fact, the knowledge and experience that "God and I are one" are central to Indian spirituality.

One of the key drawbacks of Christianity is its extreme emphasis on creaturehood and the corresponding sinfulness attributed to it. While the concept of sin has a place, especially as understood in terms of separation from God, the emphasis on sinfulness only emphasizes the separation even more. Yoga is about union, about undoing the separation, and this is why it is so appealing. At some point, we have to stop talking about the separation and embrace the idea of union, the type of union eloquently expressed in the passionate poetry of Rumi. To know the Divine in this union, we must know ourselves in the Divine image. Western Christianity teaches that we are made in the image and likeness of God, an idea that comes from the Jewish scriptures, but we are not taught how to access this image and likeness. This access is precisely what Indian spirituality offers by means of Yoga. In Christianity, anyone who seeks the high level of mystical experience that Jesus attained is looked upon with derision, even suspicion. As a result, the mystical tradition within Christianity has remained in the background and been nurtured only behind the walls of monasteries. I certainly never knew about monasticism or mysticism as I was growing up.

My Interspiritual Journey

Growing up in a conventional Christian Catholic family in India, I was attracted to the culture of Indian spirituality, but my family would have none of it. As a teen, I went to Sunday Mass as an obligation, which is why I stood outside in the churchyard with my friends and did the sort of thing most teen boys would do to stay occupied while the Mass went on. We called ourselves "outstanding Catholics."

I was nineteen at the time and attending an engineering college, which, like attending Mass, I did more to please my parents and fit into society than because of any genuine career interest. My true love was music. As a reward for attending college regularly, my parents presented me with a brand new Fender Stratocaster guitar with all the bells and whistles, and I was allowed to play with a band at the Holiday Inn for a few hours each evening.

I had always had a philosophical inclination, and this was a time in my life when I was questioning my circumstances. Why did I have privileges that so many other Indians did not have? Why did God allow people to suffer starvation and deprivation? How could I ride my motor scooter to a five-star hotel, have fun playing music, eat like a prince, and return home to my own little suite while whole families lay on the street without privacy or dignity?

One summer afternoon, I rode off to a music rehearsal with my new guitar balanced between my thighs, the body of the instrument on the floor of the bike, its neck against my own. With my right foot poised over the brake, my right hand controlling the accelerator, and my left hand on the clutch, every part of my body was engaged as I steered my way through pedestrians, buses, goats, stray dogs, and the occasional cow who refused to budge from the center of the street.

Suddenly, a car pulled out from the driveway of a school and broadsided me. Fortunately, it was traveling slowly. As it pushed the motorbike, musical instrument, and me onto the pavement, I did everything I could to protect the Stratocaster, which, incidentally, survived without a scratch. However, in the accident I ruptured the pinky on my left hand, a precious appendage for a guitar player.

I had been playing the instrument since childhood and had performed professionally since I had become a teen, earning a substantial income at that age and acquiring a reasonable amount of fame in parts of South India. Advised by doctors that sutures might prevent the nerve damage from healing naturally, I waited it out, but the process was painfully slow. During my convalescence, my father brought home books from the local library on mysticism and the monastic life. How, or why, he chose such books is a mystery. Neither of us knew a thing about the subject. Until that time, the only form of religious life I knew about was clerical, institutional

Christianity. Now, suddenly, I became acquainted with terms
such as *contemplation, mysticism, meditation,* and *monks.*

The books that my dad brought home from the library
instructed me about a marvelous inner world filled with
extraordinary spiritual visions. I read about Christian monks
in deep meditation whose faces shone with glorious light,
and mysterious subterranean chapels where they chanted
for long hours in ancient Latin. Something stirred in my
depths, and I could not help feeling that these were not fan-
ciful words of literary imagination or poetic license but
truths that had to be experienced. For the first time in my
life, I turned to the Bible with reverence and began to read
it not out of a sense of obligation, as I was used to doing,
but as a record of divine revelation and sacred mystery.

Starting with the four Gospels, I journeyed through the
New Testament, reading slowly, carefully mulling over each
sentence, and letting the words sink deep into my soul.
From time to time, I would close my eyes and listen attentively to the silences of those depths. Little did I know that
this was an ancient method of prayer known as *lectio divina,* a form of reading meditation advocated by Saint
Benedict, whose monastic order had inspired the very books
I was reading. Some mysterious transference was happening. Often, I could not read more than a few sentences.
Some of them, like the ones below, hit home.

> Jesus said to him, "If you want to be perfect, go,
> sell what you have, and give to the poor, and you
> will have treasure in heaven; and come, follow me."
> (Matthew 19:21)

> He who loves father or mother more than me is not
> worthy of me; and he who loves son or daughter
> more than me isn't worthy of me. (Matthew 10:37)

For whoever desires to save his life will lose it, and
whoever will lose his life for my sake will find it.
For what will it profit a man, if he gains the whole
world, and forfeits his life? Or what will a man give
in exchange for his life? (Matthew 16:25–26)

He charged them that they should take nothing for
their journey, except a staff only: no bread, no wal-
let, no money in their purse, but to wear sandals,
and not put on two tunics. (Matthew 6:8–9)

I lived in private quarters in our backyard, isolated from
the house, so that I could come and go without disturbing
my parents, especially since I returned from playing music
late at night. On arriving home, I would stand at the front
gate to gaze at the night sky for long periods, during which
I had hardly any thoughts, just an enormous sense of space.
Every now and then, I would find myself saying, "Help
me," and tears would roll down my cheeks. I had no idea
why I was saying those words, which seemed to well up
spontaneously from some remote place inside me. Later, I
understood this from Saint Paul's statement "It is not I, but
the Spirit who prays within me."

Eventually, I would walk to the room that had become
my hermitage behind the house. Here, I would lie on my
bed, looking up at the ceiling in a sort of trance. From time
to time, I would turn over and read the New Testament.
When the emotion built beyond a certain point, I would
get on the floor, placing my head and hands on the cool
cement. In that position, like a Muslim on his prayer mat,
I would remain still and lose track of time. It was usually the
twittering of sparrows and the chirrupy sound of mynah
birds in our mango trees at dawn that drew me out of the

posture. When I tried to move, I felt like my body had aged a thousand years.

After several weeks of living in this cocoon, I came to the clear realization that I needed to renounce the world and become a monk. Not knowing there were Christian monasteries in India, I assumed I would need to go to Europe, toward which end I was willing to sell all my possessions, including my prized guitar. For advice, I met with a Jesuit priest who sat me down and listened attentively to my story about Benedictine monks with mystical powers and my desire to become one. I told him about the subterranean chapels and the dark corridors with alcoves in which to kneel and pray, and how I would be willing to sell my guitar and other musical accoutrement that I had acquired over the years in order to purchase a one-way ticket to some desolate location in Greece or Sicily or Sardinia. But he told me about Father Bede Griffiths, an English Benedictine monk who directed a Christian ashram just 250 kilometers away.

A Christian ashram sounded right because of the Christian-Hindu combination. As a child, I had gone to a Hindu school, and I had grown up in a Hindu neighborhood celebrating all of the Hindu religious festivals with my mostly Hindu friends. It was only in my teens that we had moved to a Christian neighborhood. There was something about the word *ashram*, and the implication that Bede was a "holy man," that created in me an instant connection to Shantivanam, the informal name for the monastery. The Jesuit priest described it as a Hindu-styled Benedictine abbey.

Once I had an actual physical location to go to, a fire began to rage inside me and I became impatient. I could not wait until Father Bede replied to the priest's letter asking whether I could come. One evening in early September 1984, I announced to my family that I was renouncing the world and going off to become a monk. My elder brother fell into a rage and said I was going mad. Mother accused me of rebellion. Fortunately, Dad understood and supported the decision. My sister, whom I was close to, cried quietly.

I left that night with a spare set of the oldest clothes I could find, my toothbrush, a half-used tube of toothpaste, and some soap, all of which I placed in a worn cloth bag that hung from my shoulder. I wore a loose Indian-style shirt called a kurta and faded corduroy jeans. In my pocket were Indian rupees amounting to about two dollars, just enough for a one-way bus trip. I had closed my bank account, but unlike the great saints, I gave everything to my mom. I did not have the ashram's address, but I knew it was somewhere near the large temple town of Tiruchirapalli, about 250 kilometers from Chennai.

That night I purchased the last ticket on the last bus going to that destination and settled into my seat by the window. As I looked out at the grimy, garbage-filled bus depot, I could see families sleeping in the corners, many with children huddled close to their parents. The night was quiet, and I felt a deep peace. The bus rolled out of the depot, and we journeyed through countless little villages, street lamps dimly lighting the streets and casting shadows on houses quiet with sleeping children and exhausted parents who had labored all day for less than a dollar. I felt that I was at last going to find meaning in my life.

WE ARRIVED AT TIRUCHIRAPALLI at daybreak. Locals still refer to it as Trichy, the abbreviated form used by the British, who found the full name hard to pronounce. The area around the large interstate bus station was just coming to life. Fruit vendors were setting up their stalls, lining up colorful rows of apples, oranges, pomegranates, and guavas. Flower sellers, mostly women, were displaying marigolds, chrysanthemums, large roses, and scented jasmine. Fast-food vendors were cooking up a storm, the overpowering aromas of their spices moving through the air and mixing with the sweet scent of the flowers. I was ecstatic that morning.

I asked around to see if anyone knew of Shantivanam Ashram (the monastery in the Forest of Peace), and soon I was seated in a silver bus that journeyed alongside the most beautiful river I had ever seen. The sacred Cauvery River, also known as "the Ganges of the South," is almost a mile wide. Lining its banks are mango groves, coconut palms, and eucalyptus trees. On the other side were bright green fields of paddy, sugar cane, and thick bamboo. That morning, the river's waters shimmered as they reflected the rising sun.

This is the heartland of South India, a region held sacred not only because of the river but also because of the many historic temples located in the surrounding area. I remembered my own Hindu ancestry as I looked across the water to the opposite riverbank, where I could see the 256-foot gateway of the Srirangam temple, home to the famed Indian philosopher Ramanuja. Throughout our journey along the river, I saw young girls and women out in front of their homes creating beautiful geometric patterns with rice flour in the street. These mandalas, known as *kolams*, or "guises," are mystical designs that attract beneficial forces, blessing the threshold of one's home and inviting health, wealth, and happiness.

The bus driver stopped at a red-and-white road sign that announced Shantivanam Ashram. I knew that this was a moment of memorable significance as I stood there, looking at the unpaved road leading into the forest and feeling that I was now literally "on the path." I had also, in a sense, arrived. At the gates of the monastery, I was asked the proverbial question typical of the Benedictine monastic tradition: "Why are you here?"

"I am here to see Father Bede and join the monastery," I replied. Traditionally, to test his resolve, the monastic candidate is asked to wait outside the monastery for three days before admittance. I only had to wait a few minutes, which I did not mind in the least.

BEFORE PROCEEDING TO THE NEXT CHAPTER, I hope you have discerned by now that I have respect for Christianity and care about its possibilities. However, like you and like many other Christians, I am well aware that the tradition needs to grow, and, to its credit, it *is* growing. But with the increase of right-wing fundamentalism in America, Christians need to revisit the essential message of the gospel in view of its global implications. Such an understanding is possible only through an unbiased appreciation of the religious depth of the world's spiritual traditions. As you will learn in the chapters that follow, one can fully participate in the rich religious experience of Hinduism without compromising one's love for Christianity and without disowning one's Christian heritage. This has been my profound and personal spiritual experience.

Many Christians are not aware that Hinduism is rich in authentic and well-documented spiritual experience. Furthermore, it is rooted in the Indus Valley culture, one of the world's oldest and most advanced civilizations. It overflows with devotion and is highly evolved in spiritual practice, most notably, Yoga, which originated in the Indus

Valley between five thousand and seven thousand years ago. Steeped in liturgical ritual and backed by six major philosophies that developed as early as 500 BCE, Hinduism is also renowned for its millennia-old tradition of sacred music and chanting, which has profoundly affected my life and forms the basis of my ministry and the heart of my spiritual experience. Most important, Hinduism, right from the beginning, has been an extremely diverse tradition and holds together many contradictory forms of religious thought, which makes it a wonderful model for interspiritual dialogue. There has never been another time in human history when cultivating understanding between the world's religions and their corresponding revelations has been more important.

All too often in the past, Christians have measured other religions against Christianity on an unequal playing field, comparing the shadow side of these traditions to the light in Christianity, which was held up as the only true revelation of God. Members of other religions have done much the same. Today, however, it is time to heal this divide, particularly as Christians become more aware that there is a shadow side to their own tradition. While every tradition has a shadow, it is important for Christianity to address its own because of Christianity's enormous economic and political influence on the world. The Crusades, the Spanish Inquisition, and, in recent times, the horrific abuse by pedophilic priests, while insufficient to condemn the depth and beauty of the Christian tradition, nevertheless indicate systemic conditions that must be purged so that the divine light can shine through it more fully.

As we move toward a more balanced view of what spirituality means today, and of how we embody our spiritual presence in the world, models such as Bede Griffiths's are worth looking at for inspiration. At the heart of this journey is the universal call to mystical depth, spiritual awakening, and human authenticity. This call is being distorted by the fast-paced, extravagant, and identity-confused lifestyle of our times. We are bombarded every day by extremely powerful media sources that constantly condition our likes and our dislikes and tell us what we should want, what we should wear, and how we should behave. The spiritual journey, however, is the quest for our essence — the deepest and truest part of who we are, made in the image and likeness of the Divine, designed for eternity and configured for love. Every member of our species is invited to be a mystic, a seeker of truth, a lover of the ecstatic. We simply need new forms of spiritual synthesis and tolerance to show us how to achieve this birthright today.

2

Seeking the Essence

ALL RELIGIOUS AND SPIRITUAL TRADITIONS have a mystical core. Although Christianity, Islam, Judaism, Buddhism, Hinduism, and the many other faiths of the world have accumulated formal structures, doctrines, and the external trappings common to all institutions, each began as a way of connecting directly with the Divine presence and the vast mystery of the cosmos. Every tradition offers its adherents a path to experiencing this spiritual communion, however clouded and obscured this path may have become.

It is on this mystical plane that the vast differences between the world's religions — particularly between Western and Eastern religions — begin to dissolve. Whether you are seeking enlightenment or striving to enter the kingdom of God, the same ultimate reality is your goal, and the world's spiritual traditions offer surprisingly similar approaches to, methods for, and insights into the journey.

Having spent most of my life as both an aspiring Christian and an aspiring Yogi, I know firsthand that underneath the rituals and doctrines of these two traditions is an essential wisdom about the Divine presence. Because neither Christianity nor Yoga, especially as they are commonly taught in the West, turns its mystical face to the outside world, most people don't understand either as a tradition nurturing an internal and mystical approach to spirituality. And yet that mystical core is certainly present in both.

Christianity actually began as a mystical sect in Judaism. We should never forget that Jesus was essentially a Jewish mystic, although it is his prophetic, political, and social voice that has most been emphasized. Over time, however, an institutional superstructure grew up around the new religion, leading to the formation of doctrines and formal practices designed more to engender faith and loyalty than to engender personal communion through direct mystical experience with the Divine.

In the third and fourth centuries following the death of Jesus, many extraordinary men and women were disillusioned with what by then had become the worldly power and external religiosity of institutional Christianity, which is what happens in any tradition when the mystical dimension is underplayed. They withdrew into the remote caves of the Egyptian desert to practice an interior Christianity based on contemplation and prayer, and they sought an inner experience, a spiritual awareness of Jesus's presence and God's true nature. Going against the status quo, they refused to be associated with the Christian power consolidated by the first Christian emperor, Constantine. In this sense, they emulated Jesus, who himself refused to be associated with worldly power: "My kingdom is not of this world" is what he said to Pilate, despite the fact that saying something else could have prevented his death.

While in the first three centuries after Jesus it took great courage, deep faith, and strong spiritual practice to follow his teaching, it was different under Constantine. Now, there were benefits and incentives to being Christian. Constantine's support of Christianity was at least partially motivated by self-interest: he wanted to harness the power of the growing religion to sustain his own political power. He officially declared which texts and beliefs would be considered orthodox Christianity and which would not, all compiled by his delegated officials. While this was certainly an effective way to homogenize a wildly powerful religion abounding in mystical experience and to domesticate its power for political ends, it also suppressed the rich diversity of spiritual thought, variations of mystical experience, and the radical dimensions of Jesus's teachings. This pivotal moment marked the birth of the institutional church, which, at that time, used the infrastructure of the Roman road system and the wealth of the Roman Empire to spread its message to the world.

Reacting strongly to what they now perceived as the spiritual complacency of the institutional church, the desert mystics took to heart Saint Paul's injunction to "pray always and with all manner of supplication in the Spirit" (Ephesians 6:18). Often their core spiritual practice was to repeat a single phrase taken from scripture in order to connect directly to the presence of God. This practice developed into the complex, multilevel form of deep contemplative prayer and reading meditation that came to be known as *lectio divina*. The accounts of the spiritual progress and mystical experiences of these disciplined wild men and women, compiled and recorded by John Cassian in the fourth century, became the spiritual classic known as the Philokalia. To this

day, the Philokalia remains a vital resource in the inner life
of the Christian monk.

Roughly a thousand years before the Christian desert
mystics lived, the Yogis of ancient India found themselves
equally disillusioned with the external religion of Brah-
minical, or caste-based, Hinduism. This is why Yoga is often
presented as a nonreligion. It is not, however, nonmystical.
Like their Egyptian Christian counterparts, these silent
Yogis, called *munis*, sought the solitude of caves and forests
and mountaintops, where they could spend their time in
interior prayer. They rejected the rituals of the Hindu institution, channeling their energies directly toward the Divine presence, rather than through a priest, and offering
their breath, their life force, in place of the clarified butter
and twigs from specific trees characteristic of Hindu rituals.
In place of the *kunda*, or sacrificial fire pit, they offered the
crucible of their own hearts, and devotion as their fire.
Much like the Hebrew prophets, they proclaimed that it
was the inner state of mind and heart that was important,
not the external, sacrificial offerings.

These Indian Yogis had much in common with the
Christian mystics who would follow them. Like the desert
fathers and mothers of mystical Christianity, they rebelled
against institutional religion and sought direct personal
experience of the Divine. The most intriguing parallel, however, was that the two groups of mystics developed very similar techniques for bringing themselves closer to the Divine
presence. The Yogis' repeated use of the mantra, most commonly the sacred syllable Om, is comparable to the chanting of words from scripture that formed the basis of *lectio
divina*. And the two were used to bring about similar changes
in awareness and consciousness.

It is possible that the mantra method was propagated by those passing along the active trade routes of the ancient world, a means by which many similar practices were exchanged between India and Greece and throughout the Middle East, most notably between India and Alexandria in Egypt. This may have been how the early Christian mystics came to know of the technique.

The early mystics of the Egyptian desert weren't the only Christians to seek union with the Divine through prayer techniques very similar to ones that had arisen much earlier in India. In the Byzantine Empire, about the time that Emperor Constantine legalized Christianity in 313, there developed a mystical and monastic sect whose practitioners came to be called Hesychasts, after a word that meant "stillness" or "tranquility." They used what was essentially mantra meditation as their fundamental means of spiritual development. Hesychasm underwent a renaissance in the early 1300s, becoming a major force in the Eastern Orthodox Church. By this time, some Hesychast monks had developed elaborate and powerful techniques for attaining union with God. They combined prayer and meditation with controlled breathing and particular bodily positions — practices very similar to those of Yoga.

Instructing others in how to employ these techniques, a Hesychast monk named Nicephorus the Solitary wrote, in the 1200s, a passage that sounds similar to the language of many esoteric Yoga texts:

> You know, brother, how we breathe: we breathe the
> air in and out. On this is based the life of the body
> and on this depends its warmth. So, sitting down in
> your cell, collect your mind and lead it into the

path of the breath along which the air enters in.
Constrain it to enter the heart, together with the
inhaled air, and keep it there. Keep it there and do
not leave it silent and idle. Instead, give it the following prayer: "Lord Jesus Christ, Son of God,
have mercy upon me." Let this be the mind's constant occupation, never to be abandoned.[1]

At Shantivanam, we followed in the footsteps of all the
Eastern and Western mystics who had walked this common
path toward union with the Divine. We entered deep meditative states by focusing on repeated phrases and the movement of air into and out of our bodies. Although the form
of our practice came from the Benedictine tradition of the
Roman Catholic Church, its goal and essence were universal. An early Christian mystic, a Hesychast monk, or an
esoteric Yogi would have recognized immediately what we
monks were doing.

Our practice of contemplative prayer was based on
the *lectio divina*. As I mentioned earlier, the *lectio divina* is
a form of spiritual reading-meditation with ancient roots.
It was advocated as a core spiritual practice by Saint Benedict (480 to 547 CE), the founder of the Rule of Saint Benedict, under which Shantivanam operated.

Christian monks in the Middle Ages called their method
lectio divina, the "four senses of scripture," because they had
determined that there were different levels of listening to the
same passage.[2] These resonate with the dynamics of mantra
practice: one experiences the external audible sound (*vaikari*);
then the mental interpretation (*madhyama*); the telepathic
resonance of deep understanding (*pashyanti*); and finally,
union with the supreme state of Divine presence and Divine

mind (*para*). *Lectio* is the literal interpretation of a text, the historical context. This is like *vaikari*, the external resonance of a mantra. However, when seeking to apply this scriptural passage in our life, we attain a moral understanding of it. This is known as *meditaio*. In mantra practice, *madhyama* is the intermediate process of thought translating into action and vice versa. *Oratio*, the third variation of *lectio divina*, happens when, after constant application, we start to naturally live the teaching that is contained within the scriptural passage we have been meditating upon. There is no longer a conscious effort involved. This is what Gandhi advocated and what many Christian monks and saints practiced, as do many Christians even today. This state corresponds to the implicit and universal state of thought resonance. Good people in all cultures operate from this place, and in mantra practice this corresponds to *pashyanti*. Finally, there is the breakthrough into the state of conscious union with God that the Christian monastic tradition calls *contempatio* and the mantric tradition refers to as *para*. This ultimate state of conscious union is called Samadhi in the Yoga tradition.

Samadhi is not a state that can be produced; it is, rather, a state of grace that we enter when we let go of all else and surrender to the deepest sense of presence (or awareness) within us, which is the supreme presence of the Divine. We are created in the image and likeness of the Divine, and we realize it when a deep inner harmony is established within us. This harmony is Yoga, and we prepare for it by becoming aware of stillness in the mind and, through this stillness, consciously entering into loving communion with the Divine. Christian mystics refer to this experience as being "seized" by the Divine presence, and Yogis refer to it as "total absorption," which is what the term *Samadhi* means.

Both traditions describe this state as one in which all the activity of the mind is suspended, so that the mind can become aware of itself, as though looking into a mirror. This transparency allows us to behold a deeper reality, the God that we share. It is, in a manner of speaking, an act of coming face-to-face with God. This involves a formless nakedness in which we experience ourselves in the intimacy of God's presence. It has, of course, an implicit sexual connotation, which I explore in chapter 4.

THE CONTEMPLATIVE *lectio divina* is the essential work of the Benedictine monk, the most important part of the harmonious blend of work, study, and prayer that supports the contemplative life. The ashram I studied in followed this ideal, and Bede repeatedly emphasized that the two hour-long periods for contemplative prayer each day (one from 5:20 to 6:20 in the morning and the other between 6:00 and 7:00 in the evening) were the pillars that held up our monastic lives. Setting an example, Bede faithfully practiced each day at the appointed hours.

Early on in my time at Shantivanam, Bede suggested that I practice a particular method of contemplative prayer intended to bring a person into the intimacy of contemplation as quickly as possible. The method is simple, but by no means easy. You repeat a sacred phrase lovingly, over and over, like calling out to the beloved. This focuses the mind, challenging it to maintain a single, unified thought pattern that flows continuously toward the Divine, like a river returning to its source in the ocean. The sacred phrase, which acts like a mantra, becomes a sort of pipeline between the Divine and the human soul. Gradually the pipeline dissolves, revealing the pure union that exists eternally between the soul and its source. In other words, there is no longer any subject–object relationship, only the merging of energies into a simple union. In method and goal, this is identical to the tradition of the mantra.

Bede had me follow the instructions outlined in *A Method of Contemplative Prayer*, an obscure but succinct little book written by Father James Borst, to learn this method of meditation. Borst advocated that one do nothing more for the entire period of meditation than sit still and repeat the mantra or sacred phrase. He recommended the phrase "Lord Jesus Christ, Son of the Living God, have mercy on me, a sinner." This is known as the Jesus prayer. Alternatively, "Lord, come to my aid; God, make haste to help me" could also be used. Both of these phrases were traditional mantras of the Eastern Church, used since the time of the desert fathers and mothers.

Each morning at 5:20, I would sit down for a quiet hour in the darkness, under my mosquito net, and recite the full form of the Jesus prayer, in English: "Lord Jesus Christ, Son of the Living God, have mercy on me, a sinner." Additionally, I used, "Lord, come to my aid; God, make haste to help me." I used both these contemplative prayer phrases only for a very short period, however. As soon as I realized the power of Sanskrit, I practiced meditation with two Christian Sanskrit mantras that were derived from these traditional phrases, but without the references to sin and mercy, and I will speak about these mantras later. To be true to the Hindu culture in which we immersed ourselves at the ashram, I tried to sit cross-legged, but it was difficult to do so for such a long period as I was not used to the posture. Whenever my knees hurt, I would prop my legs up for a bit, during which time I continued to say the prayer.

At first, I struggled through the entire hour. The problem was not my knees, but my mind: it just went on and on and simply would not stop. More important, I didn't feel anything spiritual while saying the mantra. There was no glorious light, no apparitions, no angelic music, nothing — just the labor of saying the same phrase repeatedly. Nevertheless, I was able to continue with what seemed a dry and boring practice, perhaps because as a musician I had had to discipline myself to repeat the same musical phrase until I got it right. The big difference here was that there was nothing to "get right."

Slowly, I learned that contemplative prayer is a labor of love, a heartfelt response to the invitation of Spirit calling to us from our depths. Contemplative prayer is a way of reaching within to this invisible dimension of our being, and in this act we discover ourselves loving and being loved at a level and in a manner that is beyond the ability of our conceptual minds to articulate, and far more simple and direct than the love we experience through our psyches. In contemplative prayer, we learn to say the mantra not because it produces some wonderful spiritual effects but because it affirms a fundamental love relationship that is already present at the very core of our being and at the heart of all creation. Father Thomas Keating, a Trappist monk who inspires the practice of contemplative prayer (as *centering prayer*) among Christians worldwide today, eloquently describes the repetition of the mantra as an act of *intention*, the choice of the will to open and surrender to God's presence, rather than an act of *attention*.

After about a month at Shantivanam, I had the opportunity to delve deeply into a different kind of meditative tradition — that of Zen Buddhism. A Zen monk arrived from America, and I joined her in a weeklong retreat at the ashram. We practiced all morning, from nine o'clock until noon, alternating between meditation periods of about twenty-five minutes and talks and discussions of about the same length. Prior to the end of each hour, we took a short stretch break of about five to ten minutes. In the afternoon, we practiced in a similar fashion for another three hours.

The Zen monk taught me how to sit still and observe the processes going on inside me. I learned how to observe myself intensely, how to shine the light of my awareness nonjudgmentally on the continuous collage of physical sensations, sounds, smells, and feelings that rippled through my body, and on the incessant thoughts and images that passed through my mind. The key, I found, was to avoid becoming emotionally involved with any of this and to avoid mentally reflecting on the significance of what came into my mind. I learned to sit still, simply witnessing what went on without reacting or becoming involved with the content. My objective was to gain a clear, nonreactive mental vision, to concentrate fully on the present moment without suppressing anything, and without judging or labeling any part of the process as a distraction. The application of this technique gradually leads to a state of equanimity, because it centers you in the *hara*, a place deep in the belly and considered to be the seat of a person's spiritual energy.[3]

Zen is tough, and this was a difficult retreat for me, not only because I was new to the spiritual path and to meditation technique in general, but also because I had to sit cross-legged on the floor. I was compelled to abide with the pain that developed in my knees, learning to observe it until the experience of pain became fluid and impersonal.

In other words, I was not feeling the pain, but rather "a sensation was happening," and it was an experience that I didn't need to qualify or name. It wasn't pain or discomfort, just sensation, a sensation like any other. The part of me witnessing the whole process, and the experience of the sensation — particularly the nature of its vibration in the muscles and fibers of my body — were, in a sense, inseparable from one another. There was no "I" and there was no "pain," only the experience of "Zensation."

At the end of the retreat, I had a private consultation with the teacher to find out a how long it would take before my mind stopped its incessant chatter. "How long have you been meditating?" she asked. "Just a few months," I replied. "In that case," she said, smiling, "you need to wait a few years before you notice any significant difference, and it will probably be about seven years before you truly master the technique." This advice was difficult for a young, enthusiastic novice to swallow, but in hindsight it was just the right tonic for my ego at that time, which was desperately eager to make quick progress on the spiritual journey.

One day, a few months later, a well-known Buddhist monk from Sri Lanka arrived at the ashram. Everyone was excited that he was going to lead a ten-day retreat during which we would learn to meditate for long periods of time using the *vipassana* technique. The retreat ended up being a powerful meditation experience, and to this day I look back on it as one of the most powerful meditation experiences I've ever had.

The tradition of *vipassana* goes back to the time of the Buddha himself. This was the meditation technique that he perfected and taught his monks. At the heart of the practice is the ability to observe oneself and others while completely accepting everything that is part of the present moment without judging it in any way. This leads to a state of being in which one can practice loving kindness toward all creatures, or as a Buddhist would put it, all sentient beings.

Each day of the retreat was very demanding — we woke at 3:30 AM and practiced for approximately nineteen hours out of every twenty-four. The actual meditation sittings were interrupted by periods of sitting and walking meditation, which helped my knees, but we practiced mindfulness in every single conscious moment. In other words, the practice of nonjudgmental observation never ceased during our waking hours. Regardless of the task engaged in — whether we were brushing our teeth, washing our clothes, or walking — we were to remain aware of all that was taking place at the sensory level while, at the same time, refraining from all projections, labels, and descriptions. This is the practice of mindfulness.

To improve our ability to concentrate, our teacher trained us in what is known as *anapana* meditation, the art of focusing one's attention wholly on the breath so as to combine concentration and mindfulness. While concentration is an effort-oriented, exclusive task (it keeps distractions at bay), mindfulness is an inclusive process that embraces everything in one's environment without attaching itself to anything. Combining mindfulness and concentration heightens your sensitivity and helps build what might be called "mind muscle," the tenacity to keep returning to the object of one's concentration, repeatedly, without being disturbed or discouraged that one has lost sight of it temporarily. The essence of this practice — as in the practice of contemplative prayer in the Christian tradition — is loving attentiveness.

Most of our sitting meditations, and some of our walking ones, began with our chanting the famous verse, also
known as the "triple gem," sung by the Buddha's disciples
when he was still alive: "I seek refuge in the enlightened one
[Buddha], the community of spiritual seekers [*sangha*], and
the universal law of righteousness [*dhamma*]." We chanted
this in Pali, a Sanskrit-derived language used by the Buddha
to teach (which is why it is *dhamma* instead of *dharma*):
"Buddham sharanam gacchaami, sangam sharanam gacchaami, dhammam sharanam gacchaami." At the end of
each meditation session, we prayed: "May all sentient beings
be happy and peaceful." This prayer, part of the practice
known as *metta-bhavana* (loving kindness or goodwill toward all), was a means of sharing the fruits of our practice
with the world.

Shortly after the *vipassana* retreat, I experienced my first
mystical breakthrough. I was walking down the path leading to the temple when my physical body began to dissolve
— or so it seemed to me. The process happened in slow
motion, and I was distinctly aware of every nuance. The
first thing I became aware of was that I had no sensation in
my feet. My body was walking, and I could sense my legs
moving, but I could barely feel any sensation in my legs,
which were like phantom extensions. There was a translu-
cent quality to everything.

I stopped and held up my hands, which I could see but
barely feel. I looked down at my torso. Again, I could see it
but barely feel it. It was like being in a large bubble in which
I could see but could not identify any physical sensation,
just the faintest echo of it, barely enough to allow the sim-
plest muscular coordination. My body had not gone numb,
but sensation did not register in the way it normally did.

And this experience did not go away! It continued for hours and returned each day for several days in a row. During those days, I spent most of my hours in spontaneous meditation. I simply could not do anything else. Even speech was impossible. I sat for extended periods, for there was no sensation in my knees. I remember sitting in my hermitage and looking out at the tall elephant grass growing in the field directly in front, and at the vast expanse of sky beyond the river Cauvery. It was a spectacular view, and I could see it most clearly. My vision, in fact, was extremely sharp — the only sense with enhanced function.

Although I could think, I could hardly "hear" myself thinking. I understood what I was processing mentally, but I was not explicitly aware of the thoughts that were forming, or of interpreting the experience. Thoughts seemed to be happening a great distance away. It felt as if an enormous space had opened up — and it was not just inside me. It was outside, too, extending through the entire natural world within the bounds of my perception. Perhaps the long hours of sitting in *vipassana*, together with all the other disciplines I had been practicing, had produced this effect. The power of it lay in the fact that there was no getting away from it. It was simply there, staring me in the face, hour after hour.

After approximately three days, sensation slowly came back. It was something like the transition to normalcy that comes after you encounter a spectacular view. For a moment your breathing stops and your whole self is absorbed in the scene. Then, slowly, your body begins to breathe once again and you become conscious of yourself. My return to the "normal" world was similar, except that the distance I traversed was a hundred times greater.

Shortly after this breakthrough into the void — what may conceivably be understood as some variation of Buddhist *sunnyata*[4] — a man arrived at the ashram. He was dressed very simply but had an unmistakable glow about him. I never knew his name. Perhaps he was an angel.

"How are you doing in your meditation?" he asked, as though he had been following my progress from the day I had entered the ashram. As we talked, I explained the difficulty I was having in reconnecting to a sense of self after my experience of being in the void for several days.

The man proceeded to tell me about his guru, Ramana Maharshi, a great sage who was born on December 30, 1879, in the village of Tiruchuli in southern India. At the age of sixteen, Ramana had awakened to a grand spiritual experience that lasted for the rest of his life, which he lived out on the holy hill of Arunachala, about 250 kilometers from the ashram. Ramana's awakening was initiated by a sudden feeling that he was about to die. Mimicking the death process, he lay on the floor, stiffened his body and held his breath. "My body is dead now," he said to himself, "but I am still alive." In a mighty flash of enlightened awareness, he realized in all truth and fullness that he was spirit, not his body.

My mysterious mentor informed me that, like Ramana, I must discover my true Self, often written as "the Self," or Atman, as it is known in Hinduism. The ego, or individual self, he said, is nothing more than a thought or an idea that identifies itself with the body and creates the illusion that there is a mind or an individual self that inhabits the body and controls all its thoughts and actions. While the ego is built on a sense of the finite and is, therefore, ultimately unreal, the soul, or true Self, is eternal, embracing and embraced by the infinite and ultimate reality of the Divine presence.

David Godman, in *Living by the Words of Bhagavan*, explains Ramana's spiritual methodology: The "I"-thought identifies itself with all the thoughts and perceptions that occur in the body. For example, "I" am doing this, "I" am thinking this, "I" am feeling happy, and so on. Consequently, the idea that one is an individual person is generated and sustained by the "I"-thought and by its habit of constantly attaching itself to all the thoughts that arise. Shri Ramana maintained that one could reverse this process by depriving the "I"-thought mechanism of all the thoughts and perceptions that it normally identifies with, until only the Atman or the (true) Self remains.[5] Eckhart Tolle is another contemporary spiritual teacher who has succeeded in finding efficient psychological language to describe this process and teach it to others, particularly Westerners.

I had already laid the foundation for at least recognizing my true Self. I had gotten used to not thinking while I was performing routine actions such as brushing my teeth or washing my clothes or eating. I would just say a single word to identify the action, like "chewing" or "scrubbing" or "walking." This reminded me that I was to refrain from using my mind to think deliberate thoughts and to simply experience the task along with all the sensations that were part of it. Now I added to this practice a method of self-inquiry that involved asking "Who is feeling?" or "Who is thinking?" This gradually led to an acute awareness of the part of me that was witnessing everything. This eternal witness, I came to realize, is the Atman, the Spirit that dwells within us, and this is the image and likeness of God in which we are all created. God is formless essence. Our own true nature lies hidden within this essence. To help differentiate between the ego self and the true Self, the Katha Upanishad offers this:

> In the secret high place of the heart, there are two birds that sit on the tree of life: one that enjoys the fruits thereof and the other that impartially looks on.
>
> The Atman, the Spirit in us, is beyond sound and form, without touch and taste and perfume. It is eternal, unchangeable, and without beginning or end: indeed above reasoning. When consciousness of the Atman manifests itself, we become free from the jaws of death.
>
> Not through much learning is the Atman reached, not through the intellect and sacred teaching. It is reached by the chosen of him — because they choose him. To his chosen the Atman reveals his glory.[6]

The Ego and Spiritual Discernment

Walking the path toward union with the Divine and finding one's true Self are really one and the same. Those who seek spiritual joy and transcendent experience must necessarily enter into intimate relationship with this Atman, this eternal soul, this presence of God in the heart — whatever you choose to name it. This, very simply, is the essence of mystical spiritual practice and is what Jesus meant when he said, "No one comes to the Father but through Me" (John 14:6). Here, he was identifying not with his human ego but with a sense of universal Selfhood, which in Hindu terms is Atman. It is present in everyone, without exception, and is beyond name and form. What makes it a challenge — perhaps the ultimate challenge that an individual faces —

is that the ego stands directly in the way. When the ego dissolves or becomes transparent, we can, like Saint Paul, say, "It is no longer I, but Christ who is living in me" (Galatians 2:20). The Atman is none other than the Christ Self. The process of discovering it, as Jesus simply stated, is to be willing to lose or give up one's ego. Jesus asks that it be done for his sake, meaning that it be done for love, not for the sake of achievement. However, people around the world have been doing it and finding it without any association with Jesus of Nazareth. But most certainly, the Christ nature within us, which Jesus identified himself with, is synonymous with Atman.

Atman suffuses our souls and indeed the entire universe, but it remains absolutely inaccessible until the ego gives up its structures of control. Since ego *is* control (Wayne Dyer calls it an acronym for "Edging God Out"),[7] this means that the ego must fade away and, finally, dissolve. When it puts up resistance, it must be deconstructed. This, however, is not easy, for it is a direct threat to one's sense of self and personhood, because the self, the lower self, is a product of the ego. As the cultured ego begins to disappear, so too does the self — or what you've always thought of as your self — and the true Self, the higher Self, is revealed.

The ego, of course, resists deconstruction. It has spent its lifetime building up its defensive structures, and it is always ready to create convoluted arguments to protect itself and the assumptions of which it is made. You cannot make spiritual progress until you learn to recognize the operation of the ego — to become aware of its games and tricks — and understand the difference between it and your true Self, or eternal soul.

In short, one has to distinguish between the two, through spiritual *discernment*, a power that both Christian mystics and Indian Yogis have long valued. Saint Anthony the Great, one of the most revered Christian mystics of the Egyptian desert, is famous for describing the crucial value of this skill: "The gift of discernment is neither earthly nor of little account, but is, rather, a very great boon of Divine grace. And if a monk does not do his utmost to acquire it he will surely stray like someone in a dark night amid gruesome shadows."[8] In the Hindu tradition, there's a similar focus on this skill as a fundamental part of spiritual practice. The Bhagavad Gita expresses it in surprisingly similar terms, describing a practice that can be translated as the "Yoga of Discernment." Spiritual discernment is key in Samkhya philosophy, which forms the basis of both the Bhagavad Gita and the Yoga Sutras of Patanjali, considered to be among the most important Yogic scriptures. This discernment is essentially the ability to discriminate between what is real and what is unreal, meaning, the true Self and the false self, the ego. And this is why each morning at the ashram we chanted in Sanskrit, "Lead me from the unreal to the real..."

Both East and West seem to agree that the power of discernment is a gift of Divine grace. As Saint Anthony the Great says, "This [discernment] is no minor virtue, nor one which can be seized anywhere merely by human effort. It is ours only as a gift from God...and among the most outstanding gifts of the Holy Spirit."[9] The Gita proclaims, "Action without craving for the 'I' and 'mine' leads to a state of divine grace that is peaceful. Absorbed in it, everywhere, always, even at the moment of death, such a person vanishes into God's bliss."[10]

Because discernment is a gift from the Divine, you must ask for it. In both the Christian and Yogic traditions, one may request this gift in petitionary prayer. One asks the Divine for the power to discern the spiritual from the nonspiritual, the cultured ego from the eternal soul. In the Hindu tradition, petitionary prayers often take the form of mantras, which are rhythmic sounds that develop the discriminatory powers of the spiritual mind. Not all mantras are necessarily petitionary prayers, but when they are, they are essentially prayers of enlightenment. The particular mantras that address this need are often from the Vedic tradition. *Ved* means "to know" and comes from the same root as the Latin *vid*, from which we get *video* — the knowledge that comes to us through this kind of prayerful chanting comes from an inner vision, a perception, a "seeing."

Gaining the power of discernment and using it is essential for spiritual development, but it is only the first phase of the path to enlightenment (Self-realization for Hindus, awakening for Buddhists, and the anointed state for Christians). Different writers, Christian saints, and Eastern mystics have explained the path to enlightenment in various ways, but most describe a common pattern of three fundamental phases. In the Christian mystical tradition, these are called purgation, illumination, and union. Discernment is the essential work of the purgation phase, in which one gets rid of, or purges, all the ego structures that stand in the way of illumination and, ultimately, union.

The Bhagavad Gita describes a similar division when it outlines three types of Yoga. Karma — the way of purification through action — corresponds well with the purgative phase. Both embody the essential idea of ridding oneself of the barriers to spiritual progress. Next there is Gnana, the way of illumination through knowledge; and finally there is Bhakti, the way of union through devotion.

The three phases of Christian mysticism aren't linear, just as the kinds of Yoga aren't sequential or mutually exclusive.[11] Purgation often happens in fits and starts, with glimpses of illumination and even union occurring between episodes of dark, traumatic, and ultimately transformative purgation. That was the case for me during my time at Shantivanam. The mystical experience I had after the *vipassana* retreat was the first in a series of illuminative bouts preceding a purgative period that was for me very much a "dark night of the soul."

The Search for Essence

As you can see from the early stages of my monastic journey, I was committed to the central practice of the monk, which is to seek God with all your heart and soul. The word *monk* comes from *monos*, which means "alone," and this search is really a solitary search, for only we can do this for ourselves. Furthermore, the search is within, in the "aloneness" of one's inner being, although we may share a support system with others (such as in a monastery), and though we may have guides and teachers.

Zen, *vipassana*, and the Hindu method of self-inquiry contributed immensely to my spiritual life as a Benedictine monk in formation — a novice, so to speak. In fact, it was an extraordinary education, to be studying and practicing Eastern meditation techniques and opening to the spiritual language of Yoga side by side with the study of Western monasticism and the Bible.

What I learned spiritually from Eastern practices was

the value of seeking essence, which is perhaps a more meaningful word for some than *Atman*. The search for essence is the inner realization that guides our search for meaning in life. In whatever we do or say, in all that we listen to, view, and experience, it is the *essence* of these processes that truly remains with us, though we are not always aware of it. In fact, our true fulfillment lies hidden in the quality of the essence we derive from our experiences, and it is in this essence that we discover our deepest sense of meaning and purpose in life. Once we realize this, we stop being lured by superficial fulfillments that scatter our energies.

Another aspect of the awareness of essence is that it allows us to experience eternity within the context of time. Since all processes are really movements of energy in time, we begin to experience a sense of wholeness in our time-bound experiences, which become transformed into spans of eternity. William Blake described something like this in "Auguries of Innocence" when he wrote:

> To see a world in a Grain of Sand,
> And a Heaven in a Wild Flower,
> Hold Infinity in the palm of your hand,
> And eternity in an hour.

Often, we go from one thing to another without really paying attention to the amount of essence we have drawn from a particular thing or process. We can, for instance, listen to words and become so involved with the words themselves that we do not truly extract the essence of what has been said. Similarly, we can become so involved with our actions that we do not truly pay attention to the essence of what we are deriving from them. This is our predicament: we lose sight of essence! If, on the other hand, we are truly conscious of deriving essence from all our life experiences, then our journey through life literally becomes a tour de force.

In the final analysis, it is the essence of things and processes that remains with us, and these essences lodge themselves in our essence. This reaches into the realm of the Atman, the eternal image and likeness of God in which we were created. This is the heart of all mystical practice, although it is known by many names. Only within this deep experience of Self, of essence, of Atman, of the image of God, our Christ nature, does the blending of traditions truly make sense. One leads to the other, and in the process we find unity not only with ourselves but with the world outside as well.

3

Melding Traditions from the East and West

WHEN YOU ENTER THE MEDITATION HALL at Shantivanam Ashram, you immediately notice an extraordinary work of art resting in the center of the spacious red oxide floor. Carved out of a single piece of black stone, four life-sized figures of Jesus sit in meditative yoga postures inside a huge lotus flower. Each Jesus faces one of the four cardinal directions. If you are like most people, gazing at the statue leaves you completely mesmerized.

The lotus flower is one of the oldest and most important symbols in Hinduism. It represents purity, eternity, ever-renewing youth, fertility, and divinity, and it frequently serves as a pedestal-like base for representations of nearly every Hindu god and goddess. Depicting Jesus in the lotus could be interpreted as an affront to either religion, yet this work of art at Shantivanam feels completely natural and genuine. The two disparate parts merge into a harmonious whole yet retain all the spiritual power of the traditions with which they are associated. In many ways, the statue in the meditation hall represents Shantivanam as a whole. It also embodies the larger effort to revitalize Christianity with Eastern spiritual wisdom, which is why I have borrowed the statue's dual symbolism for the title of this book.

In the previous chapter, I showed how mystical traditions in both Christianity and Eastern spiritual practices offer remarkably similar techniques and pathways by which the individual, alone with God, can seek mystical states of consciousness and union with the Divine mystery. But the similarities between Eastern meditation techniques and Christian contemplative prayer mark only the beginning point in our exploration of how Christian spiritual seekers can learn from Hinduism and other Eastern spiritual traditions (and vice versa). It remains for us to reckon with the different spiritual traditions themselves — their different theologies, doctrines, symbolic systems, languages, and views about the nature of the universe, divinity, and humankind. All of this spiritual form and content matters deeply.

Form and content differ strongly between the two traditions. On the surface, it would seem difficult to reconcile the two. It was Bede Griffiths's genius not only to reconcile Christianity and Hinduism but also to do so in a way that created a harmonious whole utterly respectful of both parts. Using his heart, mind, and soul in concert, he artfully crafted ways of practicing both Christianity and Hinduism side by side, honoring both and gaining tremendous spiritual fulfillment from their union.

Father Bede's example, as embodied in Shantivanam, was so important in my own spiritual development, and so useful as a model for us to follow today, that I devote much of this chapter to describing in detail how Bede melded Christianity with Hinduism and Yoga. Everything about the ashram — its architecture, the daily routine, and the way we dressed, ate, prayed, and studied — supported our effort to be authentically Christian as well as authentically Hindu at the same time.

Father Bede was guided by the belief that, even though different religious cultures all address the same Divine source, the variety of forms matters. In other words, we need to honor the unique aspects of the various traditions as much as we need to perceive areas of commonality. Given this bedrock conviction, Bede was critical of the idea that you can use established traditions as if they were bins of raw materials from which to randomly select parts for assembling a religious practice. Such selection may be acceptable at a beginning level, but, as we have seen with the New Age movement, it reflects a childlike attempt to play at discovery rather than a mature, cohesive, and adult model. Bede believed that this kind of effort was disrespectful of spiritual traditions. Just as we should celebrate the diversity of human cultures and of Divine creation in nature, so too should we celebrate the diverse expressions of what the Divine artist has inspired in humankind in terms of worship and faith.

Assembling a hodgepodge of different religions to create your own personal one, said Father Bede, is like going to a buffet table and then mixing up all the food on your plate before eating it since it is all going into the same stomach anyway. It is much more fulfilling (and respectful of the food and the cook) to really taste the differences between the dishes and appreciate the uniqueness of each flavor. Nevertheless, that having been said, the best dishes in the world today are hybrids of cultures, refined over time and tested by the fire of passionate devotion to taste. The same can be applied to the informed and sensitive blending of spiritual symbols and practices, which is the recommended approach, and which was the approach followed by Bede and the one I continue today in my ministry.

Bede's design of the ashram and its spiritual program — like his Hindu-Christian philosophical orientation — was influenced by practical matters. Simply put, the ashram, as an official Benedictine monastery, had to abide by certain canonical rules. Not only did these rules have to be followed to the letter, but also every effort had to be made to avoid giving outsiders the impression that the sanctity of either tradition was being compromised. Fortunately, in his conscientious avoidance of syncretism, Father Bede was on solid doctrinal ground. The Roman Catholic Church makes allowances for certain indigenous forms of expression that can be included in the liturgy as long as the substance of the faith remains the same. In other words, Christian worship need not be confined to, or defined by, Western expressions alone — for instance, bowing with folded hands as a mark of reverence rather than genuflection, an act of reverence in Christianity expressed by bending down on one knee.

This stance derives from the tumultuous Second Vatican Council, which took place over a space of four years in the early 1960s. At this council, known commonly as Vatican II, Pope Paul VI opened the door to a historic rapprochement between the Roman Catholic Church and the world's other major religions. "Through dialogue and collaboration with the followers of other religions, carried out with prudence and love and in witness to the Christian faith and life," he declared, "they [the faithful] recognize, preserve and promote the good things, spiritual and moral, as well as the socio-cultural values found among these people."[1]

Melding East and West

For thousands of years, both Christianity and Hinduism have been inspiring architects and artists to create works that represent, in physical form, each religion's fundamental beliefs. The magnificent cathedrals of Europe and the elaborately decorated temples of India have special significance as concrete representations of humans' relationship to the Divine, the paths to transcendence of worldly suffering, and so on. Father Bede and the other founding monks were aware of the inspirational power of spiritual wisdom expressed in the form of architecture and art, and so they strove to make the physical environment of Shantivanam reflect their larger goal of merging Christianity and Eastern spirituality without diminishing either. The way they fused the religious symbolism from these two different but equally rich traditions in the temples, gates, crosses, statues, and other images at the ashram shows the considerable potential that each tradition has for greatly enriching the other.[2]

The chapel is a model for most of the other structures at the ashram. Architecturally and in overall form, it resembles a Hindu temple, but the symbols that adorn it are mostly Christian. A traditional Hindu temple re-creates a sense of the universe. The entrance, or *gopuram*, is very special, for through it we walk consciously into the mystery of the universe. The small *gopuram* to Shantivanam's temple shows the Divine with three faces. In the center is God the Father, as source and ground of all being; to the right is God the Son, the self-expression of the source and Divine Word; and to the left is God the Holy Spirit, mover and animator of energy, depicted here with a feminine face. Flanking this three-headed figure are two angels, guardians of the gateway. In form, this is traditional for Hindu temples: every gateway is protected by *dwarpalakas*, guardian deities who keep negative energies out of the sacred enclosure.

Beyond the *gopuram*, inside the courtyard, is the cosmic cross. This unusual symbol, which resembles a Celtic cross, is unique to the monastery. It combines elements of both Christian and Hindu cosmology. The cross itself represents the crucifixion, of course, which in addition to its central significance for Christians has meaning for Hindus — the crucifixion of Jesus is a marvelous symbol of the surrender of the ego, which is at the heart of all Indian spirituality. Superimposed on the cross is a circle, which represents the wheel of *samsara*, the Hindu cycle of birth and death. The combination of the cross and the circle gives additional meaning to the resurrection: it symbolizes that Jesus broke through samsara, and that the "way" of the cross, meaning the way of accepting suffering that is actually the karma of others, is itself a Yoga.

The *way of the cross* is a term used in Christian spirituality to point to the way of Jesus. Humility, forgiveness, and acceptance are some of the key traits of this way that he demonstrated, especially during the time of his trial under Pontius Pilate, which led to his crucifixion. All these traits are expressions of a deep level of surrender and submission to Divine will, or higher consciousness, that stem from being in love. For both Christian and Hindu, it is the surrender of the ego to higher consciousness that leads to both liberation and salvation, and this is why the "way" of Jesus can be classified as a legitimate Yoga. Liberation from the cycle of birth and death, *moksha*, is one of the chief goals of the Hindu religion and the centerpiece of the Yoga path.

In the center of the cosmic cross is the mystical syllable Om, which represents the primal Word as well as the nature of the true Self — another area of common ground between the two traditions. The cosmic cross is intentionally placed between the entrance and the sitting area so that it can represent the transformative power of sacred knowledge: armed with the knowledge embodied in the cross — the knowledge that the Word of God penetrates the veil of illusion — you enter the sitting area of the temple to seek this Divine Word in all its fullness.

In the sitting area is a stone altar in the shape of a lotus, another powerful symbol of spiritual transformation. Because this exquisite flower grows in some of the muddiest patches of earth, it signifies that divine beauty can sprout in human beings despite their darkest qualities. Additionally, the lotus links three dimensions — earth, water, and air — representing the awakened soul who is rooted in the body, whose heart flows, and whose mind is spacious. Behind the altar is the tabernacle, the small chamber that houses the consecrated host. A silhouette of Christ is embossed on the tabernacle's foot-high metal door. He stands straight, glistening in the shadowy light of the lamp, his arms stretched out wide. Behind him, instead of a cross, there is a geometric pattern, much like a sacred Tantric mandala. This Christ resembles Leonardo da Vinci's Vitruvian Man, whose symmetrical perfection models the direct correlation between the microcosm and the macrocosm, mediating between the material and spiritual dimensions of existence.

The dome of the temple is also a wonderful blend of Hindu and Christian imagery. A Hindu temple's dome, called the *vimana*, is usually adorned with images related to the enshrined deity's network of power in a cosmological context; here, the images are Christian, but they resonate with Hindu concepts. The images in the first tier symbolize redeemed humanity and redeemed creation. Saint Benedict represents the tradition of monasticism; Saint Paul stands for mysticism; Saint Peter symbolizes the sacredness of the institution; and the Blessed Virgin represents the sacredness of the feminine. Each image faces one of the four cardinal directions, a way of indicating that they embrace all of humanity. Each corner is protected by one of the four creatures from the book of Revelation: the lion, the ox, the eagle, and the angel. They represent redeemed creation. Above them is Jesus in four classic Yoga postures, depicting him as guru, Yogi, God, and prophet. The entire dome is covered in carved peacock feathers, an Indian symbol of eternity or infinity. At the very top of the dome is the *shikara*, a Hindu symbol that represents the five elements: earth, water, fire, air, and space.

Bede taught me to meditate on the symbolism of the temple structure, and I often did so before the eucharistic celebration, aware that I was entering the mystery of God, as Holy Trinity, as I walked through the gateway. Next, in encountering the cosmic cross, I empowered myself with the awareness of the Divine Word, as both Om and Logos, the luminous sound that liberates one from the endless cycle of birth and death. Finally, in joining the congregation of the faithful — my fellow monks and people from the village in community — and through the mediation of the priest, I felt myself become part of the great transformation that is eternally transpiring in the depths of the universe. In this deep place of the soul, I envisaged my participation in the creation of a new earth, in which a redeemed humanity and transformed creation are freed from the grips of time, death, and the ego.

The Monastic Schedule

Our daily schedule at the monastery was a living embodiment of the commitment to both Christian and Hindu practice. The schedule was routine, but it was far from being a dead routine, because it was based on a conception of time far older than our notion of a day broken up into twenty-four equal one-hour segments.

Brother David Steindl Rast, a well-known Benedictine monk, explains in his book *Music of Silence* that earlier generations of our human race, not ruled by alarm clocks, saw the hours of the day as being personified. They encountered the hours as messengers or angels from another dimension, representatives of eternity in the natural flow of time. And so each hour had its special significance, a unique character and presence infinitely richer and more complex than the hours in our sterile clock-time.[3] This was the basis of the ancient monastic schedule, or *horarium*, the framework that has guided monks' activities for fifteen hundred years. By wrapping our lives at Shantivanam around the monastic *horarium* and its soul-nourishing notion of the flow of time, we created a unifying foundation for our attention to spiritual matters based in two different traditions.

In the Western monastic tradition of the *horarium*, monks gather to pray formally in community at least eight times a day, in what are known as the divine offices. This is to fulfill the "work of the monk" and is separate from the individual prayer, contemplative prayer, and other types of prayer that go on during work and study. The monk prays throughout the day, no matter what task he or she is performing, in order to follow Saint Paul's injunction to the Thessalonians to "pray without ceasing" (1 Thessalonians 5:17). But during the divine offices, the whole self — body, mind, heart, and soul — is drawn into the spiritual realm in a communal setting. Communal prayer is important to the Christian, as relationship is seen to be at the very heart of ultimate reality. The Holy Trinity is a human attempt to point to this sacred dynamic in which all of creation participates.

To aid the monk in remembering his or her most sacred duty, a specially appointed "angel" announces each divine office with the sound of a bell, an earthly echo of the angels' heavenly musical instruments. In response, the monk leaves whatever he or she is doing and answers the call in love. It is like the devoted spouse who, when hearing his or her name being called, drops everything at once and says, "I'm coming right away, honey."

At Shantivanam, the first divine office took place early in the morning, before dawn. In the Western monastic tradition, this would be known as lauds, from the Latin *laudate*, "to praise." At the ashram, however, we used the ancient Hindu technique of repeating the name of God, and so we gave this office the name *namajapa*, from the word for "name" (*nama*) and the word for "repeating prayerfully or reverentially" (*japa*). In the Hindu tradition of *namajapa*, any name for God can be used, but we repeated the name of Jesus. Calling aloud the name of God is powerful in any spirituality, including Christianity, because it summons God's presence. When the name of God is repeated, as in the practice of mantra, one's awareness of the Divine presence can increase exponentially.

Every morning after the sound of the bell, the faithful would walk the sandy paths in their bare feet, slowly and reverentially moving toward the temple. Everyone, along with the birds and frogs, seemed alert to the stillness that pervaded the air before dawn. In the sanctum of the temple, Father Bede would patiently wait, seated on his wooden stool, his palms in his lap, fingertips gently touching in a prayerful *namaste*.

I have a vivid memory of *namajapa*. The sanctum is dark, except for a solitary lamp that hangs suspended from the ceiling, its light throwing soft shadows upon the tabernacle and the embossed silhouette of Christ on its door. As monks continue to file in, there is the sound of clothes rustling against skin, and of bottoms adjusting against the straw mats to get comfortable.

The tabernacle is raised on an altar composed of three stones arranged like the Stonehenge rocks. In front, and to its left, hangs the aged brass oil lamp suspended from the ceiling by a thin chain all but invisible in the darkness. Above it is a large wooden cross, laid plain and bare, a symbol of the naked presence of the living Christ and the spiritual power generated when anyone accepts pain and suffering, even inconvenience, for the sake of others. We are all aware of the energy surrounding the tabernacle: the consecrated host it contains is considered to be the actual, living, breathing, spiritual body of Jesus in his resurrected state, which is also his eternal being. To connect with the energy in the tabernacle is to consciously establish a relationship with the Divine.

Finally, there is complete silence. We hold our bodies as

still as musicians in an orchestra at the start of a symphony. Bede begins the Sanskrit chant in his Oxford accent: "Om namah Christaaya, Om namah Christaaya" — the same mantric phrase is repeated in a simple, eight-part melody cycle. Slowly, others join in, each prompted by some inner cue. Gradually, the chant takes over our energies and we rock our bodies to its rhythm.

The five-syllable Christian mantra "Na-mah-Chris-taa-ya," prefixed by the "Om," is a powerful combination, much like the Hindu "Na-mah-Shi-vaa-ya" upon which it is modeled. The Om, much like the Hebrew "Amen," is an affirmation of the Divine presence. It also represents the Divine Word, the sound by which God creates and sustains the universe, as in, "In the beginning was the word . . ." It is the Hindu parallel to the Greek Logos, the mystical Word that creates the world, and with which Christ is associated. "All things were made through him; and without him was not anything made that hath been made" (John 1:3). *Namaha* is from the same root as *namaste* — *nam* — which literally means "to bow, to bend, to prostrate" and therefore signifies worship and adoration. *Christaaya* is the word for Christ, meaning "to the anointed one." In English, then, the mantra can be taken to mean "I bow to Christ, the anointed One" or "I worship the living presence of the anointed One."

The meaning of the mantra is important, however, only when we are in the dualistic mode, when God is separate from "me." The combination of syllables is a mantra's most important feature. When we get deeper into the mantra, the syllables define the space that opens up in the mind and in the heart. Slow and mindful articulation of the syllables allows us to perceive *through* the mantra and glimpse the nature of reality, which is the Divine presence itself, unadulterated by human thought or imagination.

On this morning, as on every morning, a profound transformation takes place in each of us as we chant with devotion. Energy builds in our hearts as we plunge into deep communion with the energy field of the deity. In this particular instance, we are, as a community, propelled into the living presence of Christ, which is a distinctive energy field. Only the devotee can discern this palpable vibration, which is similar to the sense of familiarity you feel when entering your home and simply "know" that your child or lover is at home.

The chanting lasts only a few minutes in chronological time, but it is a timeless experience. As the Bible says: "For a thousand years in your sight are like a day that has come and gone, or like a watch in the night" (Psalm 90:4). Absorbed in this connection with the Divine, we all sit still and are very quiet for several minutes after the last voice dies out.

Namajapa at the ashram is an example of how Christian and Hindu practice can be fused almost seamlessly. Almost every Hindu repeats the name of his or her God or Goddess for a set number of repetitions (*purascharana*) each day (or, optionally, for a set period) as a way of continually drawing closer to the experience and presence of God within oneself. This practice of repeating the name of God has its parallel in the Christian mystical tradition, not only in the tradition of the desert mystics, but also among more recent mystics, as described in works such as *The Cloud of Unknowing* and *The Way of the Pilgrim*, both of which were written by anonymous authors. The mantra itself — "Om namah Christaaya" — blends Sanskrit and the name of Christ in the common goal of engaging with the Divine mystery.

The purpose of the mantra is to go "beyond" (*traya*) the thinking mind (*manas*) or to be liberated (*trayate*) from it. When we speak a language other than our thinking language, especially Sanskrit, which has tremendous spiritual presence and Yogic power compacted into its sounds, we are able to go beyond language and into the mystery of God. The problem with English, if it is our everyday thinking language, is that it limits our experience of God to mundane, everyday awareness. While it is important to find the Divine in everyday experience, it is only half of our spiritual fulfillment. We equally need to find the Divine in itself, beyond the range of everyday human experience, and this is why we all need mysticism, which is the search for the "hidden" dimension of Spirit.

Prayers and Mantras

After *namajapa*, we sit in silent meditation for about an hour. Then, with the golden light of dawn beginning to filter through the leaves and pour into the temple, we begin our morning session of communal prayer, which Father Bede expertly designed to bring us deeply into the mystical traditions of both East and West. Here, Bede's strategy was to divide the prayer service into distinct Hindu and Christian sections.

We begin with three long *Oms*, creating a strong resonance that travels across the four-acre ashram. Anyone, on any part of the property, would be able to feel the vibrations of the chanting passing through the body, so that even those who did not attend the service could feel the effects of the mantras. After the Om, we launch into prayers from the Vedas that connect us to the immensity and magnificence of the universe. These beautiful mantras, much like the psalms of the Old Testament, praise the majesty of God in creation. We would usually begin with the sacred Gayatri mantra, revered by Hindus as the mother of the Vedas and one of the most auspicious mantras for spiritual enlightenment. As we would chant the Gayatri, orthodox Hindus throughout the country would be looking at the rising sun and reciting the same mantra, asking the light of God to illuminate their meditation:

Om Bhur Bhuvas Svaha!
Tat savitur varenyam,
Bargo devasya dhi-mahi,
Dhi-yoyonah prachodayat.[4]

The first line acknowledges the luminous energy of the Divine, which is present in the earth (*bhur*) as much as it is present in the atmosphere (*bhuvas*); the latter is the realm that connects the earth to the heavens. *Svaha* denotes the heavens themselves, in which the Divine dwells in inscrutable light. This effulgence (*savitur*) is fit to be worshipped (*varenyam*), and its radiance (*bargo*), which is itself an emanation of divine wisdom, is invited to illuminate our meditation (*dhi*).

For many Christians, it is a big stretch to pray the prayers of another tradition, and Shantivanam was, after all, an official Benedictine monastery. Therefore, Bede, in his ingenuity, chose only those Sanskrit mantras that did not in any way threaten Christian faith but that at the same time conveyed the deepest truths and values of Hinduism. These mantras did not contain the actual names of Hindu gods and goddesses. They were universal prayers that any ardent spiritual seeker could comfortably voice while keeping in mind his or her own particular image of the Absolute. In effect, they address the transpersonal.

The logic behind this method was to get Christians to use Sanskrit, the sacred language of Hinduism, which resonates in a way that can profoundly influence the experience of prayer.[5] The sounds of Sanskrit instantly reawaken spiritual experiences that are stored in memory and cause new ones to occur; the sounds also trigger powerful energy circuitry. Latin, the central language of Christianity, can be said to do the same, but in a different way. Sanskrit awakens spiritual energy more strongly in the lower register of our energy centers (chakras), while Latin tends to stimulate the upper-register chakras. (We shall speak more of chakras later.) I loved the sound of the Sanskrit, which immediately transported me to another place inside myself, a place in which I felt inviolable, shielded by the Divine armor of love.

On this morning, other Sanskrit prayers, mostly from the Vedas, follow the Gayatri. We pray that the whole planet will be endowed with good health and happiness: "Lokah samastha sukhino bhavanthu."[6] Then, in chanting a classic prayer from the Brihadaranyaka Upanishad, we ask that we be led from the unreal to the real, from darkness to light, and from death to immortality:

Asato ma Sadgamaya,
Tamaso ma jyotirgamaya,
Mrityor ma amritamgamaya.

Our morning chanting concludes with a mantra that expounds on the fullness (*purnam*) of human experience, which becomes available to us when we are in mystical union with the Divine:

Purnamadah purnamidham
purnaath purnamudachyate;
Purnasya purnamaadhaaya
purnameva avashishyate.[7]

This mantra says that the Divine is complete in itself, and that this world is just as complete because it is pervaded by Divine energy and sustained by Divine love; and that even though the fullness of this universe comes from God, the process does not diminish God's original fullness in any way. A parallel to this mantra and the insight it conveys is reflected in the gospel passage "In Him [Jesus] all the fullness of the Godhead dwells bodily" (Colossians 2:9). The mantra suggests how the unmanifest, transpersonal aspect of the divine can manifest in a personal way in our everyday world, as in Jesus, without diminishing or altering the transcendence. It also explains how each one of us has a seen and unseen aspect that correlates in the same way: our body and personality, which express themselves in the world, and our deeper Self, our Atman, which remains out of time and space and is eternally enveloped in the divine transcendence.

We end our meditation with "Shanti, shanti, shanti," the Sanskrit word for "peace" chanted three times, to envision peace on all levels — the physical, the psychological, and the spiritual.

After chanting the Sanskrit mantras, we sit in silence for a while, absorbed in the resonance and vibrations generated by these sounds and preparing for our meditation on the Hindu scriptures. This meditation often began with a reading from the Upanishads, those beautiful texts that are the culmination of the Vedas in much the same way that the New Testament is the fulfillment of the Old Testament.

Though there are hundreds of Upanishads, the dozen or so compiled by the great philosopher mystic Shankara in the eighth century CE are considered principal. These texts, the earliest among them dating from a period between 800 and 600 BCE, are a collection of mystical writings that distill the essence of Hindu mysticism. They consist of profound spiritual discourses between enlightened teachers and their students, the fruit of withdrawal into the forest in the passionate quest of an inner reality, which is how these scriptures received the name Upanishad, from *upa* (to assist), *ni* (to be near), and *sad* (to sit). It was wonderful to hear Bede read from these ancient scriptures in the early hours of the morning, day after day. Bede was certainly a *rishi*, a seer in touch with mystical experience. I could easily imagine him as an Upanishadic figure himself, dispensing profound spiritual truths under a spreading tamarind tree.

Once we complete the "Hindu" section of the morning prayer, we make the sign of the cross and begin to pray in the Syrian Christian tradition:

> Holy are you, Oh God!
> Holy are you the strong,
> holy are you the deathless,
> who were crucified for us,
> have mercy upon us.[8]

Catholic prayers, such as the Our Father, the Hail Mary, and the Glory Be prayers, would follow. By segregating these prayers in a well-defined Christian section, Father Bede avoided any hint of syncretism. This was also a way of maintaining canonical orthodoxy while allowing us to work with two major traditions side by side, letting them inform each other, and enriching our reflections immensely in the process.

Tantric Liturgy

What followed the morning prayer may have been the most concentrated and remarkable combination of East and West at the ashram. This was Father Bede's eucharistic celebration, otherwise known as the Mass or liturgy. If you are a practicing Roman Catholic or Anglican, you know that the Mass is at the spiritual heart of the faith, and, unlike personal prayer, it is a ritual made up of a series of relatively stereotyped actions. It may seem, therefore, to be an unlikely place for incorporating elements from Hinduism.

The word *Eucharist* is derived from Greek words that mean "to offer graciously." The eucharistic celebration is essentially a thanksgiving ritual, one of loving gratitude that acknowledges the Divine's interest in our welfare (demonstrated by the self-sacrificing Jesus) and, at the same time, appreciation for our invitation to participate at the core of the Divine life. The power of the Eucharist comes from its being a ritual, something public but, at the same time, intensely personal — an experience of loving reciprocity between you and the Divine.

The liturgy is therefore not merely an enactment or affirmation of one's faith but also a powerful way of building one's relationship with God. We all engage in countless rituals to cultivate our human relationships: coffee rituals, phone rituals, movie rituals, and courtship rituals. An essential aspect of any relationship ritual is the loving attendance to detail. It is of course the quality of the exchange that matters, and most often that quality is defined by the care that goes into the preparation. In much the same manner, religious and spiritual rituals offer us the opportunity to engage in self-giving with the Divine, the difference being that we are interacting with an invisible presence. This act of self-giving turns out to be bidirectional and dynamic: the more effort and self-sacrifice we put into it, the richer the experience. In the spiritual context, each ritual act is an expression of love for the Divine presence, and through each act we open ourselves to the experience of being loved in return.

The Mass consists essentially of two parts: the liturgy of the Word and the liturgy of the Eucharist. In the first part, we make our peace with the Divine and then reflect on readings from the Bible. The second section is the ritual, which begins with the offering of gifts, peaks at the consecration, and culminates in Holy Communion. The consecration is the moment when the priest transforms the bread and wine into the body and blood of Christ by repeating the words of consecration: "This is my body [Hic est enim corpus meum]; this is the cup of my blood [Hoc est calix sanguinis meus]."

For the Christian, there is tremendous spiritual power in this proclamation: the bread or wafer is transformed into the palpable, living, breathing, spiritual reality that is directly connected, in the moment and eternally, to the presence of the Divine that lived and breathed in Jesus. This mysterious process is known as transubstantiation and is the core of the Christian mystical experience, in which one is enveloped in a state of grace and Divine mystery. When we imbibe this energy substance during eucharistic communion, we *become* the body of Christ, meaning our consciousness is transformed and we experience ultimate reality. The entire external scene — devotee, tabernacle, host — is seen as symbolically representing the soul's yearning for and adoration of the Divine presence that takes place eternally in the tabernacle of the heart. In other words, the Eucharist is a process that is going on eternally in the depths of the Divine, and every individual human consciousness is invited to participate in it by choice.

Bede had developed a Yogic form of the Catholic liturgy incorporating common elements of Tantric and Vedic ritual. On this morning, throughout the liturgy, we sit in a meditative Yoga posture, unlike the constantly varying postures — standing, sitting, and kneeling — found in a traditional Roman Catholic liturgy (which of course has its own value). For me, the extended sitting, often in the lotus or half-lotus posture, allows for concentrated attention to the deep symbolism of the liturgy and to what is happening inside me. I use Yogic muscular contractions and breathing techniques, together with hand gestures known as mudras, to work with the energy generated by the ritual.

South Indian classical music, also known as Carnatic music, expresses the hymnody during the service. For about fifteen hundred years, the Western monastic tradition used Gregorian chant in the liturgy. This type of melodic music, coupled with deep cyclical breathing, produced marvelous contemplative states for the monks. The enormous quantities of energy generated by this form of chant gave them the strength to do hard manual labor throughout the day and pray for long hours at night, on very small amounts of food and sleep. In fact, the practice of Gregorian chant qualifies as a form of yoga because of the controlled breathing, deep listening, and wholehearted devotion entailed in it. The use of ancient Carnatic music during the liturgy at Shantivanam produced comparable amounts of energy in the chakras, the body's vital energy centers.

The most important variations from the traditional Catholic version of the liturgy occur at the consecration of the Eucharist. The priest sprinkles water around the stone lotus altar to consecrate the space and the ritual. Then he places eight flowers (representing the eight directions of creation) around the bread and wine (symbols of the body and blood of Christ), chanting, each time he places an item, a Sanskrit mantra pertaining to a specific aspect of the risen Christ. For instance, he may chant: "Om ishaaya Christaaya namaha" (Lord and Christ, we worship you). The congregation responds with: "Namo namaste Christo namaste" (Christ we adore you).

Next, the priest waves incense and fire, clockwise, around the bread and wine, representing the infusion of divine energy into the process. Incense represents the presence of God, while the fire represents the creative power of the Divine. Finally, every person witnessing the ritual anoints himself or herself on the forehead with sandalwood paste, consciously consecrating his or her own body and blood and offering them for transformation into a spiritual reality.

I had never experienced the Eucharist in such a manner before coming to Shantivanam. It felt authentically Christian, yet authentically Hindu, and I was drawn into the mystery of Christ in a way that did not require much effort on my part. What affected me most of all was an underlying current, a sense of vibration, pulse, and presence that moved and swelled, or contracted, throughout the service, as though it were alive. This opened the way to communion, which, of course, is the purpose of the entire service. At this focal point, there is a definite sense of crossing over into another space, another dimension. At Shantivanam I understood, for the first time, what it was to be Christian. Even though all the cultural nuances were authentically Indian and Yogic, I could actually taste the essence of the tradition that had flowed through the souls of the great European mystics, such as Meister Eckhart, Mechtilde of Magdeburg, and Saint John of the Cross. I felt connected to the same vital undercurrent that had rippled through the hearts of thousands upon thousands of devout Christians over two millennia, and I felt it strongly enough to trace the energy back to the original wave that had inspired the first apostles to follow Jesus as rabbi, as teacher.

What was perhaps most amazing to me about experiencing the Eucharist in this manner was how it awakened energy in my chakras. I could often feel palpable pulsations, expansions, and movements of energy in various parts of my body during the service. Some of this energy was most certainly sexual, and during the liturgy I often felt as if I were engaging in a sort of lovemaking with the Divine.

It should not be surprising to hear the Mass described in this way. Even the traditional liturgy can be understood through the lens of sexuality, not in any crass, undignified manner, but through sublime, metaphorical analogy.[9] The consecration, after all, is about engaging in communion with the body of Christ. At Shantivanam, the incorporation of Tantric ritual into the liturgy brought out more clearly the sexual aspect of the Mass. Tantra teaches that primal sex energy is the foundation of both human sexuality and spiritual practice; the body is therefore sacred because it is the physical expression of primal sex energy. In these terms, the consecration is a powerful Tantric proclamation, and Jesus's body on the cross is an explicit Tantric image. Jesus offered both his body and his sexuality in a dramatic act of selfless cosmic love, and he did this in full awareness of the collective human ego and its manipulative shadow aspects. The celibate monk, priest, or nun in Christian tradition seeks to do the same and can learn to use methods of Tantric yoga to offer both body and sexuality in the deepest experiences of prayer and meditation.

Expressions of Hindu and Yogi spirituality were scattered throughout the remainder of our daily routine, always in a way that felt both authentic and perfectly compatible with the Christian framework of our monastic lives. Before every meal, for example, we chanted in Sanskrit:

Hare Yesu, hare Yesu, Yesu Yesu, hare hare;
hare Christa, hare Christa, Christa Christa, hare
hare.

This beautiful chant in praise of Jesus (Yesu) is metrically modeled on the famous Maha mantra, or "Great mantra" ("Hare Rama, hare Rama, Rama Rama, hare hare; hare Krishna, hare Krishna, Krishna Krishna, hare hare"). While the meter is the same, the words *Yesu* and *Christa* transform the chant into a Christian mantra.

After our meals, we chanted a beautiful prayer from the Bhagavad Gita:

Aham vaisva naro bhutva, praninam deham asritaha;
Prana apana sama yuktah, pachami annam chatur
vidham.

In this prayer, the Lord, as Spirit, declares, "I (*aham*) become one with the life force (*prana*) that pervades the body. Mingling with the upward and downward breath, I digest the five kinds of food in four different ways." The five kinds of food are sweet, sour, salty, pungent, and bitter. The four ways of consuming them are chewing, licking, swallowing, and inhaling. If you have ever eaten Indian food with your hands, you know that this grace is most appropriate.

The Three Pillars of Indian Culture

Father Bede believed that explicitly spiritual practice was not the only arena of our lives as monks that could be deeply enriched by what the East had to offer. Those learning to be monks were given the opportunity to study three pillars of Indian spiritual culture — Sanskrit, Yoga, and Indian classical music — with outside teachers who traveled to the ashram to offer lessons.[10] Once I had settled into the rhythm of the ashram lifestyle, I began to study all three.

I began my Hatha Yoga training with Shantikumari, whose name means "princess of peace." This gentle soul was a devout Christian nun drawn deeply to Hindu spirituality. In response to her calling, she had traveled to the Himalayas to study at the ashram of the famous Yoga master Swami Sivananda. Shortly after my beginner's-yoga training with her, she entered a five-year period of silence and solitude. I was fortunate to have her as my first teacher.

Our Hatha Yoga classes were held in the meditation hall known as the Dhyana Mandir, a large rotunda supported by eight granite pillars marking off the directions of creation: North, South, East, West, Northeast, Northwest, Southeast, and Southwest. The word *dhyana* means "meditation," and it is the seventh step in the eightfold path to liberation espoused by the great Yogic sage Patanjali in his classic system of Raja Yoga, meaning "the Noble Path." This was the path my teacher Shantikumari followed, and she embodied every branch of that eightfold path in her life, both on and off the mat. In the morning, we practiced stretches and yoga postures for an hour and a half. Shantikumari was keen on a full twenty minutes of *yoga nidra* at the end of our practice. Swami Satyananda Saraswati, founder of the Bihar School of Yoga, describes the practice of *yoga nidra* as a systematic method of inducing complete physical, mental, and emotional relaxation while maintaining awareness at the deeper levels.

This Yogic discipline is practiced while lying flat on the floor, face up, with the body angled symmetrically. In the first phase, you progressively relax your muscles by moving your awareness through different parts of the body. This is followed by an awakening of sensations through contrasting pairs of opposites: for instance, by tensing and contracting muscles in an area till all muscle groups are covered. The last phase is a visualization technique using rapid images to mobilize energy in the cells while the body itself is at rest. The whole practice is so relaxing, yet so energizing, that you come out feeling more rested than you do after a good night's sleep, and with more than enough energy to get through all of a day's tasks.

Morning yoga postures included sun salutations, several variations on the triangle, spinal twists, the plow, shoulder stands, the fish, the cobra, and headstands. In the evening, the emphasis was on Yogic breathing, *pranayama*, together with various Yogic concentration techniques, such as gazing at the tip of your nose, or at a burning flame (*trataka*), for a full twenty minutes. These methods of making the body supple, harmonizing the breath, and focusing the mind greatly improved my ability to concentrate on the mantra during meditation.

In the late morning, Kalaivani, a young music instructor from a well-known music institute, came to teach the basics of South Indian Carnatic classical music. Carnatic music is spiritual at its heart: every note is considered sacred, and so is every musical scale, which can also be either masculine or feminine. Even poetry has musical and spiritual significance in India, where the rhythms of poetic meters are compared to spiritual horses that transport us into the spiritual domain, creating a direct link between the soul and the sacred. Above all, the voice is seen as the ultimate expression of spirit, capable of plunging us deep into the heart of mystical knowledge. Education in Carnatic music is itself a profoundly spiritual process, with extraordinary symbolism and devotion built into every facet of the pedagogy.

Indian music has its origin in the Vedas in a form of psalmody that is approximately three thousand years old. The Sama Veda, one of the four principal Vedas, literally the "song" Veda, laid the foundation for Indian music. During the singing of the Veda, the vocal recitation of mantras during the ritual sacrifices was often accompanied by musical instruments, particularly the *veena*, an ancient stringed lute that is the precursor of the sitar.[11] The history of South Indian music officially starts in the Sangam period, which stretches back to the beginning of the third century CE. During this time, a great confederation of tremendously creative poets and musicians burst onto the scene. This music met with challenge, but also grew, during the Muslim invasions that marked what is called the medieval period of Indian music, which began in the seventh century and ended with the close of the fifteenth century. Also known as the Bhakti period, this was a time when music and poetry stimulated great devotion throughout India, and Hinduism's deepest philosophies were propagated in the vernacular. The modern period of Indian music began in the sixteenth century and continues today. In this most recent form, it is multidimensional, at once musically rich, philosophical, and religiously contextualized for both musician and audience. The music at Shantivanam was grounded in this rich and powerful tradition.

Previously, my training had been in Western music. Furthermore, my entire approach to music was based on performance, on impressing others with my talent. At the ashram, music became a means for me to connect with God and to become aware of the sacred dimension of all life.

In the afternoons, Mr. Parthasarathy, an elderly Brahmin gentleman from the nearby town, arrived to teach us Sanskrit. Before any studies commenced, we always chanted: "Sahana Vavathu, Sahnau Bhunaktu, Saha veeryam karvavahai, Tejasvi na vadhi tamastu ma vidvisha vahaihi." The mantra asks that we (student and teacher) be protected and nourished as we work together with great vigor, that the fruits of knowledge obtained be shared equally between us, and that there be no dissension among us. For thousands of years, Indians have chanted this prayer at every gathering where the sacred is taught. My spiritual schooling in India often took place in the open, in the shade of large trees, similar to the settings in which the great seers of the Vedas, as recorded in the Upanishads, shared their wisdom. I can still recall sitting in the cool shade of the mango groves and reciting noun declensions that put me in a trance.

I had studied Sanskrit in Hindu school, so I was familiar with the alphabet and basic grammar; studying the language in the context of the ashram, however, revealed to me its full spiritual depth. Everything about it, actually, was spiritual. Even the rules of joining words and consonants together, a process known as *sandhi*, is a spiritual methodology that reflects the merging of energies, as in Yoga. When Sanskrit became a written language (between 800 and 1200 CE), the script was called Devanagari, "the city of the Gods," because each letter of the alphabet was seen as an abode for the Divine spirit. The name for this alphabet, *varnamala*, means "garland of shapes and forms." The vowels of the Sanskrit language are called *matrika*, or "mothers": they are considered sacred feminine powers that birth life through our words.

In my book *The Yoga of Sound: Tapping the Hidden Power of Music and Chant*, I mention Hans Jenny, a Swiss doctor, artist, and researcher who invented a variation on the oscilloscope called the tonoscope, which could make the human voice visible without any electronic apparatus as an intermediate link. This instrument yielded, for the first time, the amazing opportunity to see the physical image of a vowel, tone, or song produced by a human being. In a fascinating discovery, the tonoscope revealed that, when the vowels of Hebrew and Sanskrit were pronounced, the shapes configured by the substances used in the equipment resembled the written script symbols for these vowels. Imagine the deep sensitivity and inner vision of these two great cultures!

Comparing the Traditions

It would have been impossible for Father Bede to have integrated authentic elements of Hinduism and Yoga into the spiritual practice and physical symbolism of the Christian monastery had significant commonalities not existed between these Eastern traditions and Christianity. In this chapter, I have already pointed out many areas of such compatibility, but there is value in collecting these and others in the same place. With this in mind, I offer the list below, which is by no means complete.

These short descriptions only skim the surface, of course. Each topic could be the subject of a whole book by itself. In the chapters that follow, I discuss several of these areas of potential mutual enrichment in greater depth. As we explore further what Eastern traditions have to offer Christianity, you will see that in some cases the two traditions are remarkably similar, whereas in others they diverge considerably but remain compatible nonetheless. In general, you will find that, if you approach each tradition with respect for its essential wisdom, the apparent contradictions begin to dissolve. And most important, you begin to see that Eastern spiritual philosophies offer new perspectives that may help you perceive and experience the living truth underneath what has become (for many) dead ritual and inflexible doctrine.

- The Hindu conception that ultimate reality contains the elements of Brahman, Atman, and Purusha is similar to, and compatible with, the Christian idea of the Holy Trinity. In both cases, the three elements are all fundamental, interrelated, and inseparable. The supreme Brahman is considered the ground of all being and is analogous to the ultimate mystery of God, whom Jesus called Father. Atman is the spirit of Brahman present in the human being, which Christians can relate to as the "image of God," in whose likeness we have been created. The idea of Purusha as the Great Cosmic Person — who is the very soul of the universe, and "through whose primordial sacrifice the universe came into being"[12] — is strikingly parallel to the mystical body of Christ described by Saint Paul. While the Purusha Sukta emphasizes the cosmic dimensions of the divine personhood in the birth of the universe that gives form to a great diversity of ways of being, the mystical body emphasizes the personal fulfillment of consciousness in and through creation in a mode of being in which all diversity is unified, for "there is neither Jew nor Greek, there is neither slave nor free man, there is neither male nor female; for you are all one in Christ Jesus" (Galatians 3:28).

- Both traditions emphasize the importance of establishing a personal relationship with the Divine based in mutual love. While in Christianity there is communion, which is the experience of oneness in relationship and the climax of the eucharistic celebration, there is, in Hinduism, the experience of *darshan*, the experience of seeing, and being seen by, the Divine that is the climax of the temple experience. Both communion and darshan are about direct contact, the former seeking a union that emphasizes relationship, and the latter seeking a union in which all sense of individuality is lost and there is total fusion to the point of identification.

- Eastern forms of enlightenment — realization of the Self in Hinduism, awakening in Buddhism — are similar to the anointed (Christ) state of Christianity. In all three approaches, there is a surrendering and transformation of the ego. The Eastern (Hindu and Buddhist) way is very much about the human movement toward the Divine. In the Christian (and Jewish) approach, the Divine is reaching out to us.

- Mystics in both the Hindu and Christian traditions have laid out similar paths to achieving the enlightened state. The stages of purgation, illumination, and union described by Christian mystics could be seen to correspond to the three Yogas of the Bhagavad Gita — Karma, the way of purification through action; Gnana, the way of illumination through knowledge; and Bhakti, the way of union through devotion.

- Hinduism and the Judeo-Christian tradition have had similar historical or developmental trajectories. In both, the focus has moved from the external to the internal and mystical, and then to the transcendent, as evidenced in the sacred writings of both. The Hindu progression from the poetic mantras and complex rituals of the early Vedas to the introspection of the forest yogis and the great spiritual breakthroughs of the Upanishads closely parallels the earliest psalms, rituals, and prophets of the Old Testament that paved the way for the revolutionary teaching of Jesus.[13] This development is evident in the way the sacred texts of both traditions are organized: the Vedas lay out rules and rituals as the Old Testament does, while the Upanishads, with their focus on enlightenment, compare with the New Testament. In both instances, the latter texts are seen as fulfillments of the former. In addition, Jesus and the Buddha played remarkably similar historical and spiritual roles in their respective traditions: Jesus, during his life, sought to reform the Jewish tradition in much the same way that the Buddha (and the Yogic tradition) sought to reform Hinduism.

- As a great spiritual teacher who attracted disciples, Jesus played a role very similar to that of the enlightened Yogis whose knowledge is distilled in the Upanishads. The Upanishadic Yogis (also known as *rishis*, or "seers") withdrew to the forest in their passionate quest for an ultimate reality, and, through spiritual discourses with their students, transmitted their profound insights. Many of Jesus's great statements echo some of the *mahavakyas*, or "great utterances," of the Upanishads. For instance, the essence of "I and the Father are one" (John 10:30) can be seen to echo "Aham Bhahmasi," or "I am Ultimate Reality," from the Brihadaranyaka Upanishad (1.4.10), as well as "Ayam Atma Brahman," which can be translated as: "The ground of my being and the ground of the universe are one and the same" (Mandukya Upanishad 1.2). Additionally, Jesus's use of parables helps people who are stuck in the details of religion to move into the spirit of it, or in Eastern terms, to move from dualistic to nondualistic consciousness.

- There is an intriguing parallel between the seven chakras envisioned in Hinduism and Yoga and the seven mortal sins and seven cardinal virtues of Christianity. Each of the seven sins can be seen as an action or thought that blocks the upward movement of energy in a particular chakra, while the virtues are a type of yoga that facilitates the openness and flowering of that energy center. Viewed the other way around, the conception of the chakras as energy centers linked to the rising of energy necessary for joining in union with the Divine offers a way of seeing the Christian notion of seven mortal sins in a new, enriching light. There are also parallels between the chakras and the seven sacraments, which Caroline Myss develops brilliantly

in her book *Anatomy of the Spirit*. I discuss these parallels further in the next chapter.

- The spiritual ideals of both traditions — the ideals of
  Self-realization and liberation on the one hand, and
  salvation and forgiveness on the other — have similarities and valuable differences. These speak to human
  fulfillment despite being part of different visions of
  what that fulfillment is and how it is achieved. I discuss
  this in the epilogue.

WHEN WE LOOK AT HUMAN HISTORY within the context of
evolution, we see movements, and within these movements
are landmarks, moments of profound change and growth
that have shaped the flow and direction of energy, information, and life. The births of stars, the appearance of the
first amphibians, and the extinction of the dinosaurs are
events as powerful as the discovery of fire and the invention
of the wheel. The births of the major spiritual traditions of
the world are as important as any of these.

Interestingly, Hinduism does not present itself as historical, as Judaism and Christianity do. Hinduism is really
sanathana dharma, "the eternal order of the universe," and
it does not originate with any individual human or human
community. The realization of the highest consciousness,
which is also Self-realization, is at the heart of this movement.
Evolution in creation is cyclical, an eternal birthing of ages
and universes that spring up from the navel of Brahma (the
creative power of the Spirit) and that are sustained by Vishnu
(the preserving power) and destroyed by Shiva, only to be
created, sustained, and dissolved all over again. Brahma,
Vishnu, and Shiva are all aspects of the one Supreme Brahman. The purpose of creation is *lila*, or "sport," or simply the

joy of being creative that is intrinsic to the Divine nature. Meaning is derived from knowing the power behind this process, Brahman, the one indivisible unity that serves as the continuum for all existence. If one does not awaken to the mystery of Brahman, one can become lost and deluded, possibly even destroyed by the cycle of birth and death. However, the spark of the Divine within the human has many opportunities to be reborn and to awaken over many lifetimes. Self-realization is ultimate fulfillment; it moves one out of the realm of time and penetrates the illusion that one has an individual existence separate from Brahman. The East functions with this perspective.

The Jewish and Christian traditions look at evolution from an eschatological viewpoint, seeing it as a linear motion in time that is leading toward a definite fulfillment. God is actively present in human history and is purposefully guiding it toward a definite fulfillment in which all the suffering of humanity will find ultimate meaning. Our life and our choices are unique and powerful, and how we exercise our will in this life determines our joy in eternity, which is often viewed as an extension of time. This places a lot of responsibility in the hands of the human. *Love* and *justice* are the key words. The Western world functions with this viewpoint.

Both viewpoints — Eastern and Western — have value. While the Bible shows how one can engage with the world while transforming the ego, the Eastern scriptures teach how to disengage with the world and awaken to spiritual reality beyond the ego. The individual who can embrace the two and hold these seemingly paradoxical perspectives in balance may be the prototype for the future.

4

Finding Unity with the Divine

HINDUS SEE A GRADUAL DECLINE IN DHARMA, or righteousness, in each of four cycles of creation, and in each age the Divine takes form (such as that of Krishna or the Buddha) to keep alive the power of righteousness and reconnect estranged humans to the highest consciousness. Christians and Jews see this estrangement through the lens of a dramatic turning point expressed in the Garden of Eden story. In both, Christianity and Judaism, there are ways to return home. However, the insights and methods of Yoga can greatly help and enhance the process.

At some point in our evolution, humans became self-conscious — aware of our individual existence, separate from the Divine essence and the rest of creation. It was a momentous turning point that gave us tremendous power and freedom. Instead of being automatons, we got to exercise our free will, make choices, and shape the world as we wanted. There were some costs, of course. No longer invariably protected by God, we were compelled to fend for ourselves, to labor and to toil, and, hardest of all, to learn responsibility.

Self-consciousness (in this case ego consciousness) had another important consequence: separation from God. In this state of dualism, we were no longer enfolded in the loving embrace of the Divine, as were the other creatures of God's creation. Since the beginnings of self-consciousness, humans have felt this separation as a huge void in our hearts and souls. So, while we have capitalized on the freedom and power of a dualistic existence, we have also been yearning to heal the wounds resulting from this existence, to experience once again the oneness with God.

The Christian story of Adam and Eve is about grappling with this fundamental loss of wholeness and its consequences. Eden is a metaphor for the primordial wholeness that existed before the dawn of self-consciousness: the apple is self-consciousness;[1] "the fall" is the permanent exclusion from Eden that we suffer as a result of being self-conscious beings. We've obscured this deeper symbolism by focusing on the notion of sin and by thinking of the fall as wholly negative. However, once a year, at Easter, Christians briefly remember the positive side, proclaiming, "O happy fault, O necessary sin of Adam, which gained for us so great a Redeemer!"[2]

The fall from Eden was really a form of empowerment, because the self-consciousness that separated us from God also gave us the power to choose. We fell so that we could rise even higher — into a state of unity with the Divine more mature and fulfilling than the primal wholeness we lost, because it is an informed, or enlightened, unity. This is why there is no going back to the primal state of Eden: we can only go forward into enlightened unity. Through the grace of our fall, we are given the power to rise, but we must choose to rise, want to rise.

Why did the serpent tell the two primal humans to eat the apple so that they could become like God, especially when they were already created in the image and likeness of God? What we may infer from this paradox is that in God there is a mature sense of unity in diversification, and it is *this* state toward which the serpent was propelling Adam and Eve. The human being must progress — consciously, through the exercise of personal choice — toward the restoration of unity as an act of will. This is why the state of spiritual enlightenment can never be taken for granted.

When we choose to rise, we align ourselves with the Divine force, and this fuses our will with that of the Divine. Our capacity for choice is the ultimate gift of Divine love. Without it, we would simply be safely programmed automatons, doing the will of our Creator. Free will enables us to consciously and deliberately choose or reject the love of the Divine.

The central message of Jesus, "Repent, the Kingdom of God is at hand" (Matthew 4:17), is the invitation to participate in what the Divine intends for humanity, the journey toward consciously chosen unity. In repenting, at least in the general sense of the word, we acknowledge that we have at times exercised our power to reject love. To reject love creates pain — the pain of separation, the loss of connectedness. To repent, then, is to take the first step toward restoring harmony, balance, and connectedness to the most fundamental relationship — that between source and expression, God and creature, matter and life, being and consciousness. In this sense, Yoga is a meaningful act of repentance, for it is a wholehearted effort to restore harmony between the Divine and ourselves.

Happily, God has always remained the source and sustainer of our existence, despite our estrangement. Spirit has never abandoned us. God, in the voice of Krishna, declares in the Bhagavad Gita: "Whenever righteousness falters and chaos threatens to prevail, I take on a human body and manifest myself on earth."[3] Throughout history, the Semitic traditions have witnessed that the Divine is always forgiving and ever ready to receive us. This is the heart of the Christian revelation, and the Jewish tradition too: that God actually chooses us and is interested in the reciprocity of our love. The most moving aspect of the Christian revelation is the sense that ultimate reality is vulnerable, that it has created us out of love and wants us to interact with it out of complete freedom of choice, risking the possibility that we will not so choose.

The reciprocal, mutual love that can fuse the individual with God points to, and flows out of, an eternal relationship at the heart of all connectedness, governing even the attraction between atoms, between molecules, and between cells. Jesus came to reveal that God is in relationship with every human being and seeks reciprocal love. This is why the Bible says that to clothe the naked is to clothe God, and to feed the hungry is to feed God.

The Hindu tradition has the same sense of relationship and communicates the Divine's yearning for us. Krishna, the voice of God in the Gita, says, "Give up [surrender] all actions to me; love me above all others."[4] In India, the Divine is also in every guest who comes to our home; to feed him or her is to feed the Divine. Relationship involves freedom, which is the power to respond in love or to reject the other. When we choose God, God chooses us. The Gita puts it this way: "However men [and women] try to reach me, I return their love with my love."[5]

While in the Hindu tradition, the lack of dharma is in the individual, the Bible's story of Adam and Eve teaches that humankind's fall was collective. This implies that all humans share the responsibility for healing the resulting divide, but it also contains the message that each individual healing and internal healing has proportional collective consequences and external consequences. As each individual reconnects to the Divine and repairs the damage done by living in dualism — which manifests variously as personal neglect, societal abuse, and unconsciousness — the whole world enters into a more harmonious relationship with the Divine. In this context, it is easy to recognize that the life, death, and resurrection of Jesus can be seen as the Divine effort to atone for collective human karma so that all of humanity can begin that restorative journey toward ultimate union.[6]

The human race as a whole is increasingly ready to undertake this journey. Just as an individual separates from his or her earthly mother and progresses through the stages of life, learning to exercise choice in giving and receiving love, so we as a species get to pursue an ever-more-mature relationship with the Divine as part of our evolution. We are progressively more capable of consciously choosing a relationship with the Divine suffused with reciprocal love.

For the individual, however, entering into intimate relationship with the Divine is not just a matter of choosing to do so. It also requires work — and this work centers on transforming the ego, which, paradoxically, is part of the gift of individual consciousness that makes it possible for us to choose the path of unity in the first place. This transformation of the ego is the goal and the challenge of spiritual practice. It is a process that the Greek Orthodox tradition calls *theosis*, or the "spiritualizing of the human person." Not surprisingly, something very much akin to *theosis* is the central message of Yoga too. In both Eastern and Western spiritual traditions, then, there is a sense that you *earn* your enlightenment, your union with the Divine, and that you move in that direction because you truly want it for yourself and for the world. The doctrine of karma establishes the momentum caused by our choices when we either accept or reject love. However, *after* the fact, you realize that your every effort toward the good was blessed by Divine grace, and that it was just the repeated choice that was ours and ours alone.

The Role of Sexuality in the Spiritual Process

Whenever we use the word *union*, the reference to sexuality is immediately implicit. Sexuality is one of the most powerful metaphors that we have available for describing and understanding the deepest experiences of the mystical journey and the unitive relationship that we seek with the Divine. In accounts of the experiences of many Christian mystics, the relationship with God is called a "marriage" and its bliss is spoken of as "ecstatic." The poetry of Rumi, the Song of Songs in the Bible, and the love poems of the Hindu saint Mira Bai are all representative of the connection of sexuality and romance to spiritual experience and union with God.

Part of the power of sexual analogy is that it goes beyond the metaphorical. Union with the Divine really does involve a form of the same energy that we think of as sexual.

This is why sexuality is such a profound part of who we are as humans. The reason that sexuality and romance in film and in marketing are so powerful is precisely that they reflect the fundamental love and energy connection we have with the Divine. In the pornographic industry, this power is exploited and perverted to the extreme.

Bede Griffiths often spoke of sexuality as the fundamental love instinct in human nature, put there by God and itself divine in its essence. However, the spiritual nature of our sexual energy can be easily corrupted by the ego and its structures, as evident from the roaring success of the pornographic industry. Yet, underneath this corruption is a pure, unsullied mystical process that comes from the heart of Divine love.

Bede taught that our sexuality should be neither suppressed nor indiscriminately indulged. To utilize its power for spiritual ends, he said, you consecrate the energy. To *consecrate* one's sexual energy is to lovingly offer it to the Divine, to allow it to become part of the mystical process. Consecrated sexual energy is channeled, accepted, honored, and nurtured; its movement through every vortex in the body is welcomed and celebrated.

The Hindu tradition offers us a healthy and insightful way of understanding the role of sexual energy in spiritual practice.[7] Like many of the other spiritual traditions of the East, the Hindu tradition identifies an omnipresent creative energy that acts as the cohesive and moving force of the universe. In Western Christianity, this force is comparable to that of the Holy Spirit (in Hebrew, *ruah*, or "breath of life"), though many Christians are not comfortable with this comparison. In Hinduism, *shakti* is the broad term for such a force. The word *shakti* means "energy"; the great goddess

Shakti is the personification of energy, or shakti. In Yoga, the manifestation is *prana*, the life force within the breath. In Tantra, the shakti manifests in the human body as a psychospiritual force called kundalini (and the goddess Kundalini is the personification of this force). Normally, kundalini lies dormant; it is envisioned as a serpent coiled at the base of the spine (the Sanskrit word *kundal* means "coiled"). Awakened kundalini has enormous potential for moving a person toward spiritual enlightenment.

Kundalini has a direct relationship with sexuality. The two are often thought of as different forms or expressions of the same essential energy. As long as kundalini remains inactive, sexual energy animates the body on the physical plane. But when sexual energy is sublimated and consecrated, directed toward the goal of union with the Divine, it can awaken the coiled serpent of kundalini, a symbol of latent Divine power. Energy needs to move, and it keeps moving, even in the celibate monk and Yogi. But when it is not moved out of the body through normal sexual activity, it is moved inward and transformed into the sacred energy of kundalini, provided it is not repressed. Consequently, one way of understanding kundalini in the human realm is as the combined power of sacred and sexual energy awakened out of our passionate love for the Divine and the Divine's passionate love for us. As such, it is far more potent than sexual energy alone.

For kundalini to realize its transformational potential, it must move upward in the human body. From its dormant position at the base of the spine, kundalini has to be coaxed upward, stage by stage, in what may sometimes be a painful and effortful process of purification. As it rises along the spine, kundalini grows in intensity until it reaches the top of the head, where its outpouring produces a spiritual awakening

and realization. This physical and energetic pathway is analogous to a psychological and spiritual development.

The successful rising of kundalini in the individual —
represented as its emergence from the top of the head — is a
well-documented experience in the Yogic tradition, and innumerable texts exist on the subject. Working with kundalini
is also the central component of the Tantric Yoga tradition,
which is concerned with the movement and intensification
of spiritual energy. But those who practice Eastern forms
of meditation are not the only ones who experience this
type of energy awakening. Many of the mystical experiences
described by Christian saints and hermits bear a strong
resemblance to classic emergence-of-kundalini experiences.
Saint John of the Cross and Saint Teresa of Avila, for example, describe mystical experiences that seem identical to
kundalini awakening. Even the experience of the early church
at Pentecost — fire descending on the heads of the disciples
— may be construed as a form of kundalini.

In the past few decades, many Christians in the West
have experienced surges of energy that can be described in
terms of kundalini. Philip St. Romain, a present-day Catholic
who experienced an intense spiritual awakening as a result of
contemplative prayer, is one who has written about his experiences and compared them with the emergence of kundalini.
The lack of resources and references to support Westerners
who undergo such powerful spiritual experiences led to the
creation of the Kundalini Research Network in 1990. While
some individuals who experience kundalini practice Eastern
meditation techniques, others practice Christian prayer, and
some do not practice any form of prayer or meditation what-
soever. Consistent with this is the fact that the halo — easily
seen as a representation of kundalini energy emerging from

the top of the head — is a near-universal symbol of sanctity, present in artwork depicting both Christian saints and Hindu deities and holy men. The experience of kundalini emergence would seem to be universal.

From this vantage point, we may boldly declare that the mysterious energy of kundalini has been a part of all sacred traditions around the world since the dawn of human history. This sacred energy has in fact been the force driving evolution since the origin of the universe.

When kundalini awakens inside you, it takes the form of an arousal, a movement of energy that begins from deep within and then encompasses your whole being. Again, there is that strong sexual reference. It is almost as though something alien enters your being. You feel it in your bones and your muscles, but it is not just physical; there is simultaneously an otherworldly quality to it. Here I speak from personal experience, because after some months at the ashram, kundalini began to awaken in me.

As a result of my spiritual practices, I had begun to experience what I thought of at the time as a tremendous increase in sexual energy. Being a celibate monk, I was able to use my knowledge of Hatha Yoga and my understanding of kundalini to channel this energy toward spiritual ends. It wasn't easy, but I was committed and passionate about the process. I used a combination of *asanas* (yoga postures), *mudras* (hand gestures), *bandas* (muscular locks), *kriyas* (dynamic movements), and *pranayama* techniques (controlled breathing) to move this energy toward the top of my head. At least, that is what I sincerely tried to do. I awoke at 3:30 AM to practice yoga for ninety minutes before going to the temple for *namajapa*. Additionally, I practiced one hour of yoga in the evening before meditation.

After a few weeks, this discipline bore fruit. I began to experience strong surges of energy in my body. There were hot flashes, lights, and powerful sounds like large drums beating in my head. Sometimes, an enormous flow of energy would come from the back of my head, accompanied by the sound of a waterfall. At other times I would feel as if my body were on fire. All the pores in my skin seemed to open up, and intense heat radiated from them. Then there were tingling sensations, millions of pinpricks deep inside the body, as though my internal organs were being tattooed. It was a powerful experience.

There was also a downside. For instance, there were a good many times when I developed a tremendous heaviness in my body. I felt as if I was carrying a dead weight around. Then there were times when I would eat enormous quantities of food, even after I was full. My stomach would be packed tight, like a suitcase zipped beyond capacity, my skin taut across my navel. Or I would experience an insatiable craving for sugar. Someone gave me a bag of éclairs during that time to distribute to the community, but I found myself uncontrollably consuming all fifty of them. Another time, I consumed three jars of jelly all in one sitting. Obviously, the control I was exercising over my energies needed compensation!

The movement of kundalini upward from the base of the spine to the top of the head deserves a closer look, because it is a powerful way of describing the essence of spiritual practice and the route to union with the Divine. In Western mysticism, the symbol of the ladder is analogous to that of the spine in Yogic mysticism. In the human body, kundalini rises through seven different levels, which Eastern spiritual traditions have long characterized as chakras. *Chakra* comes from a Sanskrit word meaning "wheel," and accordingly, a chakra is often described as a spinning wheel, as a center or vortex of activity where life-force energy is received, transformed, and expressed. Each chakra has a particular location along a vertical line extending from the area between the genitals and anus (the root chakra) upward to the top of the head (the crown chakra).

Most fundamentally, each chakra relates to a particular set of physical, emotional, and spiritual needs in the individual. The root chakra relates to our sense of security and survival; the sex chakra pertains to reproduction and regeneration; the power chakra, located in the gut area, controls our individuality and therefore our individual power; the heart chakra affects our capacity to love and to relate to others; the throat chakra controls creative expression; the third-eye chakra, located between the eyebrows, oversees wisdom and insight; and the crown chakra, on the top of the head, is the channel for enlightenment or Divine union. It doesn't take esoteric insight to see the common sense of these associations.

Understood this way, the chakras can be connected to psychological processes, components of one's being: physical illnesses result from denying or suppressing the spiritual realizations that the chakras are created for. In traditional Hinduism as well as in contemporary therapeutic disciplines, the chakras are related to different gland secretions, sounds, and colors, and many Western therapists and medical doctors are now using the chakras as a healing framework. While such integration is only just beginning, it promises great value in its development, especially when it is used in combination with Western models of healing. Healing and spirituality are two sides of the same coin, and this is yet another important aspect of the marriage of Eastern and Western processes.

The chakra system can also be related to various developmental progressions. At one level, for example, the chakras can be compared to the stages of human life, from life in the amniotic fluid (the root chakra) through childhood, puberty, adolescence, adulthood, parenthood, and old age. At each of these seven stages of life, energy begins to awaken in the chakra that governs that phase. We might see a particular chakra dominating each of these phases in human development, and this insight can guide us in creating meaningful rites of passage as well as lead to a greater understanding of our spouses, children, and co-workers.

The chakra hierarchy can also be seen as mirroring the evolution of the human species. Prehistoric humans existed at the level of the root chakra, concerned mostly about security and survival. Next followed a period of magic and mystery. Today, humans — collectively speaking — have advanced to the stage of egoic consciousness associated with the power chakra. This is the mass consciousness, located at the third chakra. This implies that collectively we have four more phases to go. Although we see tremendous creativity, deep philosophical insight, and profound awakenings in many human beings, we cannot say that the majority of our species have achieved maturity and fruition in the higher chakras. In fact, we often see whole societies regressing to lower chakra mentalities today. Maturity and fruition in the higher chakras are imminent, though, because the rate of acceleration of our collective progress has increased exponentially. And, as a result of our strengthened global communications network, our conscious maturation and movement to higher chakras on a mass scale can happen quite rapidly. This is the great hope and the thrust of the modern spirituality movement, and it is what we are counting on in the Age of Spirit: that the masses will rapidly advance to the fourth, fifth, sixth, and seventh chakras. When all of humanity arrives at the seventh level, the fulfillment of God's plan will have been reached. Then, we will be, quite literally, in the New Jerusalem, where Christ is all things in all people. This is how the Eastern vision of the chakras can be meaningful to the Christian and vice versa.

At the cosmic level, the progression through the chakras describes the evolution of the universe. From the original big bang (the opening of the universe's root chakra) to the formation of stars and galaxies, we see the development from intense heat to expanding energy and matter. From all of this, biological life evolved, and it is now evolving a refined consciousness, which in turn will lead to the enlightened unity we have been speaking about. While in the East this unity is seen as taking place on the individual level, the Western spiritual traditions see it as collective, and so yet again, we see the value of combining these views.

Today, we are gaining increasing clarity about the chakras and their role in physiology, consciousness, and spirituality. Through the phenomenal work of such teachers as Caroline Myss, for example, we are beginning to understand that the chakras are psychological energy storage centers that link to hubs of crisscrossing nerve ganglia in the body, and that the body's glandular secretions relate to specific psychological states associated with those nerve centers. "Our biology is our biography" is a new scientific cliché, and it echoes an ancient Eastern understanding of the chakras.

The many layers of meaning embodied in the chakras help us understand the upward movement of kundalini and its association with spiritual awakening. In one sense, kundalini awakening is a natural and organic unfolding of evolutionary consciousness. In its dormant state, lying coiled like a snake (a reptile) at the root chakra, kundalini corresponds to the most primitive stage of evolution, represented in the human brain by the brainstem, the so-called reptilian brain. (Here again is a biblical parallel with the Garden of Eden.) It is part of the natural order of things for kundalini to rise out of the root chakra and follow, in the individual, the same upward path it has followed in human evolution. In recognition of this natural tendency, some Hindus refer to the awakening of kundalini at the base of the spine and its movement through the chakras as "Shiva dancing backward to the Source" — the source being Shakti, the goddess who is identified with absolute being or ultimate reality and seen to reside at the top of the head. This natural tendency of kundalini to flow upward through the course of an individual's life span also seeks to "flower" or maximize its potential as each chakra is activated — hence the classical imagery of open flower petals that generally increase with each ascent.

Yet despite this upward pull, kundalini doesn't move of its own accord and it is often inhibited by patterns and habits that are either normal to a particular phase in human development or being excessively controlled by the ego. For many, the greater portion of this energy is released through the sex chakra, where it is expressed as libidinal energy, while the rest of it passes through the power chakra and so on, becoming progressively less apparent in the subtler centers. In the spiritually awakened person, it is just the opposite. The greater amount of this energy finds expression in the subtler chakras. For it to be converted and expressed as sacred energy, kundalini has to be coaxed up the spine, slowly but surely, through the sexual organs, abdomen, heart, throat, and third eye, until it flowers in the seventh chakra at the top of the head. This involves considerable and conscious spiritual effort, and the physical organs are simply the physiological references for psychological and spiritual advancements. Without the corresponding psychological and spiritual maturity, the energetic realizations by themselves can easily result in a powerful ego trip, as we have seen in some Eastern teachers and New Age experts.

Returning to the Garden of Eden analogy, this process can be thought of as a matter of repairing, at each successive level of your being, the damage caused by the Fall, the original separation from Divine love. At each juncture or chakra, you must consciously restore the balance of cosmic order and unity associated with that level. Your gut, your heart, and your mind must be purified in turn so that kundalini can ascend. When kundalini breaks through in a final release at the crown of the head, it becomes possible for the final healing — of the separation between you and God — to take place. Accordingly, both the Western mystical approach of purgation, illumination, and union and the Eastern path of Yoga are both part of the evolutionary process of developing spiritual energy in our individual and communal lives. The two traditions have a common goal and process, and each contributes its own valuable insights.

It is not merely a coincidence that the Christian tradition identifies seven mortal sins (also known as the seven deadly sins), and that the Hindu tradition has seven chakras through which kundalini ascends. Each of the seven sins relates to a way of being or thinking that blocks the passage of sacred energy at one of the chakras. Here is a great example of how Christian teaching can contribute to the Eastern chakra system. The sin of greed, which can be seen as an overindulgence of the basic, root-chakra need for security and safety, keeps sacred energy stuck at the root chakra. Lust, the desire to use and manipulate another purely for self-gratification, prevents spiritual progress by trapping energy at the sex chakra. Gluttony, which arises from the unsatisfied needs of the gut-based, ego-driven power chakra, stops the movement of energy in the lower abdomen. Anger (wrath) impedes spiritual growth by blocking energy at the heart chakra. Anger also stems from an unwillingness to forgive and forgiveness forms the centerpiece of Jesus's teaching. Laziness (sloth) inhibits the movement of energy by stunting creativity in the throat chakra. This finds expression in the lack of initiative to engage in spiritual practice and spiritual effort. The sin of envy obstructs spiritual progress by impairing the wise and intuitive perception of the third-eye chakra or by judging others or by being spiritually competitive. Jesus taught that "the lamp of the body is the eye: if therefore thine eye be single, thy whole body shall be full of light" (Matthew 6:22).[8] Finally, the sin of pride and arrogance — also known as the sin of angels — stands as the final barrier, at the crown chakra, to ultimate union with the Divine. As you can see, here is a marvelous example of how Yoga and Christianity can combine to bring moral power to each chakra advancement.

In the East, the emphasis in Kundalini Yoga is on the energetic and metaphysical dimensions. By bringing the traditions together, we can have a stronger and more meaningful system. For instance, in the Christian tradition, the spiritual destruction caused by the seven sins is balanced by the practice of the seven contrary virtues: pride is overcome through humility, envy by kindness, sloth through diligence, anger by patience, gluttony through abstinence, lust through chastity, and greed through liberality and sharing. Sharing was the first teaching practiced by the early Christians, and the entire Christian church was built on its power. In other words, there is a healthy first chakra at the root of the church. However, this has become obscured by centuries of power and wealth and bureaucracy. A famous joke illustrates this point: A young man from a third world country seeks to join a Western monastery. Overwhelmed by the tour of the rather plush environment, he exclaims, "Goodness gracious; if this is the poverty, I wonder what the chastity is like." Nevertheless, sharing and caring for those who are less fortunate continues to be a strong and noteworthy Christian practice.

The practice of combining the virtues with knowledge of the chakras can be thought of as a Yoga of the Christian tradition, a "way" that deals with the blockages in each chakra caused by sin.[9] However, the Catholic Church's many legal problems related to sexuality in recent years have made it clear that the church has neglected the proper development of the second chakra, the sexual center, and this is what needs work today. Yoga, and much of the knowledge of working with energy that comes through it, can contribute greatly to the health of this chakra as well as inform the overall development of the spiritual journey among practitioners in the church, not to mention those who have left it and seek meaningful ways of reconnection.

Chakras and Sacraments

Christianity's seven sacraments, as Myss has pointed out, also have a connection to the chakras. Each sacrament can be seen to have a strong relationship with a particular chakra, and each is designed to ensure that the individual maintains a connection with the Divine — which, energetically speaking, is a matter of sustaining the flow of sacred energy. We can say that, through the sacraments, Divine grace is given the opportunity to channel into each chakra at a specific stage in an individual's life, during a period when that particular chakra is most dominant. The sacraments are evolved rites of passage that ancient cultures used to help in the development of the chakras in an individual's life. In this light, they are "spiritual initiation rites" for the divinely guided development of each of the chakras. However, for many today, the form that the Christian sacraments take, and the language used to interpret these profound rituals, is no longer relevant. Again, the incorporation of Eastern spirituality, Yoga, and meditation techniques can help to enhance and revive the power and relevance of the sacraments for those Christians who no longer feel connected to the existing forms of the tradition. Following are some possible interpretations.

Baptism, which is a symbolic immersion in the waters of the unconscious, helps awaken a person to his or her true identity in God, an identity that is distinct from the ego, or false self, offering the profound security that allows the flow of sacred energy from the root chakra. This is the awakening to the true Self in Eastern cultures. It would be helpful if the practice of meditation or contemplative prayer were introduced to baptized individuals to help them regularly nurture the Christ Self within. Confirmation could be seen as the phase when a person is initiated into the love of God and begins to learn to consecrate the energies centered in the sex chakra and direct them toward ultimate fulfillment instead of indiscriminate sexual gratification. Some simple

Tantric techniques could be taught to help the individual control and sublimate sexual energy. After penance or confession, the forgiveness of God offers a spiritual empowerment that helps free a person from the tyrannical and self-absorptive power of the power chakra–based ego. This, in the East, is somewhat comparable to the surrender to a teacher, the guru, who mediates, much like the priest, to bring light and freedom into the soul of the practitioner. At this stage, working closely with a spiritual director who also has knowledge of Yoga can be very helpful.

Holy Communion can be viewed as the sacrament of the heart chakra, one that enables a person to discover in himself or herself the fundamental love that already exists in relationship with the Divine. Here, the method of contemplative prayer can be developed further into deeper states of mystical union. In matrimony, the partners can learn to develop the creative energies of the throat chakra together and, in this way, build community in the world. Marriages often break up because of a breakdown in communication, which is directly related to the throat. Additionally, methods of working with sexual energy, such as through yoga practice, can be introduced to both partners, so that intimacy need not be too heavily conditioned by sexual exchange alone.

Through the sacrament of taking holy orders, a person is recognized as someone who will minister to others. This call to selfless service comes from the higher wisdom of the third-eye chakra. Although the term *holy orders* formally applies only to entry into the priesthood, we can extend its meaning to the choice of any vocation, honoring that moment when one's profession becomes a true form of service. Holy Orders is also a sacrament that can be used to honor elders who have amassed substantial spiritual experience in their lives. Finally, there is the anointing of the sick, the sacrament also known as extreme unction, in which a dying person is anointed with sacred oil and prayed over to ensure safe passage through death into eternal life. Because oil is a powerful symbol for energy, especially consecrated energy, there is a direct connection here between East and West that can be developed further in the administration of the sacrament. In the East, *sannyasa*, or final renunciation, is seen as the ultimate goal of every human's journey, and this renunciation is to be expressed, ideally, before physical death and in preparation for it. Elements of *sannyasa* could be introduced to Christians who are in their elder years to offer them added insight into the spiritual value of that phase.

In this manner, or in some comparable way, the seven sacraments can become a powerful system of self-transformation for Christians by enabling them to tap into the value of wisdom-based spiritual traditions, including the wisdom streams within Christianity. In this context, *wisdom tradition* refers to spiritual knowledge used for self-transformation, in contrast to, but in partnership with, faith and belief structures.

Mystical Experiences and Mystical Union

There are many paths to union with the Divine. Participating in the sacraments, observing the seven virtues, practicing Kundalini Yoga or Tantra,[10] and engaging in the various forms of meditation and contemplative prayer can all bring you closer to the unitive state by dismantling the barriers to oneness and opening the energetic connections between you and ultimate reality. They are all means to the same end, and they are honorable and powerful means precisely because they share this goal. However, by combining methods of the East and West — that is, by combining methods of active confrontation and passive purification — we can effectively achieve what Father Thomas Keating calls the "dismantling [of] the false self."[11]

It is helpful, though, for us to keep in mind that, even though there is only this single goal of union with the Divine, it has at least as many manifestations and levels as the paths one can take to achieve it. Furthermore, it is neither a fixed goal nor a state you enter into once and for all. You can glimpse it, stand on the threshold of its infinite expanse, and then have it fade away. There is, in the East, a notion that ultimate breakthrough is permanent. I, however, feel that, even after profound breakthroughs, there is an inner mechanism that relates to our power of choice that must continue to choose (albeit unconsciously) to be in relationship with the Divine. Perhaps the continuousness of this choice provides some semblance of permanency,[12] but the possibility of making a different choice at some point remains very real. This is why no level of enlightenment can be taken for granted.

At the ashram, I had the experience of drawing tantalizingly close to feeling the immediate presence of the Divine, only to drop back into a state of spiritual barrenness. At first I had the mystical experiences of altered consciousness that I described earlier. I then progressed to having more intense episodes, during which I lost all sense of control over my body and mind.

There were many occasions, particularly as I lay down to rest (which was always on the floor), when I would feel an electrical energy enter my feet and slowly work its way up my body till it reached the top of my head. It was a vibration, a throbbing feeling accompanied by a dark, smoky effect that looked much like the night sky. This happened to me at all hours of the day and night. One night when this energy had seized my body, I felt somewhat frustrated about not having control, so I gave a great push and felt myself sort of ooze out of my body. I could discern the dimensions of my hermitage clearly as this happened. I reached out for the light switch against the wall, and even though I could "feel" it, I could not turn it on. In that moment, I realized that I was not in my physical body.

I gave another push and went through the closed door of the hermitage and out into the open space. There, on the porch, I could see the field of elephant grass waving in the moonlight and the Cauvery flowing in the distance. The color was vivid, extraordinarily bright, and everything was sharp, as on high-definition TV. I tried to go around the ashram grounds in this altered form but found it difficult to move, so I returned to my body. There was a jarring sensation as I entered it, as though I was getting into a shrunken suit that no longer fit me. My body was still penetrated by the electrical energy that had occupied it when I left. I accepted the situation and tried to sleep, but I was stunned by the out-of-body experience. I knew this was my dream body, or astral body, and it was fascinating to have had such an intimate experience of it. It never happened again.

Then there were experiences of sound translating into color and vice versa. One day, I was sitting on the stairs of the library, waiting for the noon angelus bell to sound. When it did sound, I could see ribbons of golden light curl around the temple and come toward me, accompanied by a dull, thudding sound in the distance. It shocked me, so I closed my eyes and waited for the next peal. Same thing! In the darkness of my inner vision, I could see those gold rib-bonlike waves moving toward and past me. It happened again for the third bell, and for the long volley that announced the angelus. I waited, stunned, and it happened a fourth time, as the bell sounded for noon prayer. It happened for the last time when, during the light-waving ceremony, the ritual bell (a different size and timbre) was rung inside the sanctuary. This time the circular golden waves rippled out of the sanctuary as though stones had been plopped in a still pond. I can still remember the whole experience with exceptional clarity.

Although these were amazing experiences indicating much more than the awakening of my spiritual energy, they didn't add up to what I intuited was spiritual union with the Divine. I was able to perceive the underlying reality of existence, but I was not enfolded in the Divine's loving embrace in a way that permitted me to sense the Divine as distinctly other than my awareness. Additionally, I knew this at the time, because I did not feel true fulfillment. Eventually I became aware of what was missing: I had not entered into authentic *relationship* with the Divine. The structures of my ego were still standing in the way of the necessary surrender.

My situation at the time can be explained through a classic analogy offered by Father Thomas Keating in the prologue to his book *Invitation to Love*.[13] In the early stages of the spiritual journey, says Keating, the structures of the ego are like a stained glass window whose flaws are revealed when the light of faith (the experience of God) filters through it. In the second stage, the ego is more like transparent glass: the light comes through clearly, but there is still a filter, something between you and the light. However, since that filter is colorless and shapeless, you can fail to notice it. This was the stage I had progressed to. Still ahead lay Keating's third stage, in which the glass is completely shattered, allowing the pure, unmediated, unfiltered light of Divine consciousness to fill one's being.

5

Charting a Path

GOING INWARD TO FIND THAT PLACE where God dwells is a journey with many challenges. Although the trials and obstacles we face on the journey have some common sources, each person faces a different set of challenges and overcomes them in different ways. Making your way around the obstacles in your search for spiritual truth is, therefore, more like wandering through a labyrinth than treading a straight or well-worn path. But with each success, breakthrough, or new insight, you make progress in the largest sense of the word, even if enlightenment feels as far away as ever.

What we have as our primary guide on the journey is our inherent spiritual design. It is the why and how of our being, and it is always with us, in the now of our existence. If we have lost sight of this Divine source, it's only because of our education in this world. Starting in our childhood and then throughout our schooling and career, many, if not most, of us have been taught that the world is a dangerous place, that we must compete with others to be successful, that others are out to get us, and that our race and our community are different from and better than others. In addition, in order to function effectively in the world, we have all spent much effort developing, strengthening, and honing our egos. Learning to exercise healthy caution and building a sense of self in the world are important, but if you are like most people, these aspects of your development have gone far enough to have obscured and suppressed the spiritual self that has always been inside you.

As long as our spiritual self remains suppressed, attempts at spiritual practice are likely to be frustrated. When our methods of prayer don't seem to produce the results we expect, our ego steps in with its judgment to make us feel dissatisfied, setting in motion that wheel of self-doubt that almost ensures the results won't be what we want. We have to remember in such situations that we are dealing with years of negative conditioning, which has given us habits, thoughts, and impulses that push us to look for love and spiritual fulfillment within a narrow mental framework. The German mystic Meister Eckhart described the problem well when he wrote, "God is at home [within us]; it is we who have gone out for a walk!"[1]

As we progress on the journey toward reconnection with our spiritual design, we don't necessarily need to look for teachers outside ourselves. Our pain and the condition of our souls are ready to teach us much of what we need to know. Even more powerful is an archetypal force at work in everyone's life that has been called the "guru principle." Although the guru principle can take the form of an actual physical person or guru (the word *guru* translates as "that which dispels the darkness"), it more commonly shows itself as a spiritual presence or interior awareness that works through books, dreams, inanimate objects, or other people.

One of the most important lessons I've learned in the many years that have passed since I first walked through the gates of Shantivanam is that the most potent enemy we face on the journey inward is our very own ego. In chapter 2, I explained that the ego masquerades as the core of our self by creating the "I" and preventing us from recognizing our true Self, our spiritual essence — the interior manifestation of the Divine that Hinduism calls Atman. In Christianity, this is the Christ Self, the anointed self. As Saint Paul would say, "It is not I, but Christ who lives in me" (Galatians 2:20). However, the Christ Self can shine only with the cooperation of the ego. Achieving a certain "transparency" of the ego is what spiritual practice is truly about. This is the *theosis*, or spiritualizing of the ego, that we spoke of earlier. I find this more helpful than the typical Hindu approach of treating the ego as an illusion, something that is to be destroyed altogether. However, there is value in understanding what is meant by *illusion* in the East.

From the Hindu perspective, the world of the senses and the constructs of the mind are both illusory: they are merely surface phenomena in a constant state of flux, below which lies a permanent level of existence, the infinite reality of the Divine. It is the ego's function to make you identify with the illusory physical and psychological worlds; this identification keeps you trapped in them and out of touch with the underlying reality and with your true Self. This is why Patanjali, in his opening sutras, describes Yoga as the control of the mind's flux. The purpose of Yoga, he explains, is to enable the true Self to shine forth. As long as there is flux, the self is identified with the mind's content, and that is precisely what fortifies the ego (Yoga Sutras 1:2–4).

Discovering the absolute dimension of existence requires that one break through the illusion, or maya, created by the ego. The ego fights this process, of course, but it may do so indirectly, by taking responsibility for every bit of spiritual progress, every outward manifestation of greater holiness. When this is happening, your practice may actually be strengthening the ego rather than transforming or dismantling it.

After I learned the powerful methods of meditation and contemplative prayer, experienced mystical states of consciousness, successfully channeled kundalini (for the time), and received considerable praise from Bede Griffiths for my spiritual discipline, I was poised for more profound breakthroughs. What stood in the way of further progress, and remained there for quite some time, was my ego.[2] I had developed what you might call a spiritual ego. I was proud of the simplicity of the life I had embraced — my bald head, my ability to sit in the lotus posture, and the rigorous fasts I could undertake. This wasn't the overt, gloating pride but the subtle, sophisticated kind. I was also proud of the powerful breakthroughs I had had so early in my spiritual development, my prowess with Sanskrit and Indian music, and so on. Yet underneath it all, I felt emptiness and an unfulfilled longing, because I was not yet ready to jettison my ego — the part of me that drove me through the whole process so that it could receive its strokes. I have recognized this same dynamic in many of my students and other people I talk with, and, of course, I continue to observe its operation in my own psyche even now. Recognizing it and transforming it is my constant practice.

While there is a certain value in Christianity's emphasis on the ego's "sinful" nature — and the ego is sinful in the sense that it is the main cause of our "separation" from love — the emphasis can be problematic when it continues to articulate this separation during times of deep meditation and mystical union. The other extreme occurs in New Age spirituality, which seeks to indulge the ego in spiritual matters in a manner that often fails to challenge its power to remain the center of attention. This self-absorption can be limiting, because it prevents true self-transcendence and an authentic recognition of the deeper Self. With Eastern spiritual methodology, there is a third extreme, and that is the vision of an annihilated ego that can easily result in denial of actual egocentricity.

This is one reason why the marriage of Christianity and Yoga is important. Taken by themselves, Yoga is in danger of becoming self-preoccupied, and Christianity too self-denigrating. Brought together, the two traditions can help create a better balance between sanctity and mysticism. I will return to this thought later.

The self-discipline of spiritual practice — fasting, meditation, prayer, yoga postures, and so on — can be a powerful way of transforming the ego, of deconstructing its complex structures. The basis for this is really the refusal to indulge the ego and its routine program of "I need this now." Denying the ego immediately makes us aware of its presence, its power, its need to control, and its self-interest. This perception can offer us great insight into the complex construct of being that we are — a mix of ego, soul, and spirit — and bestows upon us the grace of a discriminating awareness. This, in itself, is extolled as a type of Yoga in the Bhagavad Gita, namely, the Yoga of Discernment.

The cunning ego, however, can turn self-discipline to its advantage. It may create the delusion that a strong ego merely calls for even stronger modes of self-discipline and self-denial. One may build a supremely ascetic lifestyle, forgoing sex and other pleasures, fasting regularly, meditating for long hours — all the while only reinforcing the ego's structures of self-preservation. "I am doing so well in my self-denial!" we may think, naively. "It is only a matter of time before my ego dries up and blows away." However, even after profound spiritual breakthroughs, the ego can and does rebuild itself.

What must accompany spiritual discipline is, therefore, an acceptance of the need for a deep, radical surrender. Surrender is hard to describe. It is a way of relinquishing our will within its own nature, allowing it to dissolve into the power that keeps it functioning — a divine power that is our spiritual core and that is hidden in the depths of our being. As Father Keating artfully states, "The chief act of will is not effort but consent."[3] This intuitive process involves a trusting awareness of the interior presence of spirit, and the willingness to surrender control to this presence, not by effort, but through submission. Quite simply it means giving up control as well as the desire to control. The more complete the ability to relinquish control, the more radical the surrender. By combining loving discipline with heartfelt self-surrender, we can marshal a potent means for truly deconstructing the ego.

For most human beings, it is not possible — or even necessarily desirable — to become permanently free from the structures of the ego. Having lived with an enlightened being, namely, Bede Griffiths, and having observed many great spiritual teachers from close proximity over the years, I can honestly state that I haven't seen any of them completely free of ego, meaning that its crafty head shows up every now and then. Enlightened people are not egoless, but they have a more transparent ego that allows the true Self to shine through. This is why it's important to understand that ego structures are a necessary part of our functionality in the world. Just as the body is an extension of the mind, the structures of the ego can function as scaffolding for the soul. So if the ego is shattered, it will reassemble itself, using the spiritual breakthrough that shattered it as the raw material for weaving new modalities. The ego's deconstruction, meanwhile, has provided the soul with a benchmark reference, which remains, even if the ego regenerates, giving you a healthy perspective on your ability to rise beyond self-limiting perceptions.

This is why, even after a spiritual breakthrough, regular spiritual practice and a constant effort to evolve are crucial. The lives and times of many contemporary Eastern teachers in the West have clearly demonstrated that even the most significant metamorphic experiences can become corrupted if enlightenment is taken for granted. Just as the body's cellular structure is constantly being regenerated through healthy DNA, the structures of the ego are also being constantly regenerated by something comparable to DNA in the realm of the soul. Spiritual practice, coupled with surrender, fortifies healthy soul DNA, which in turn regenerates healthy ego structures. Conversely, the lack of spiritual practice, or spiritual practice without meaningful surrender and continuing spiritual discrimination, can cause unhealthy soul DNA to regenerate unhealthy ego structures, ones that are self-destructive. I learned this lesson well from the example of Bede Griffiths, who meditated faithfully each day despite his palpable holiness.[4] I've seen the same in all the great spiritual teachers. Even Jesus himself prayed regularly.

Another important way to keep your soul DNA healthy is to practice sanctity. Following the mystic path comes naturally, in the sense that we are all called to be mystics — that is, we are all invited to know the hidden Divinity that resides in us, in each other, and in all of creation. The path of sanctity, however, demands that one go further. In addition to knowing the Divine within, we also seek to embody the Divine in the world. One can be a mystic without being a saint, but every saint is necessarily a mystic because sanctity is mysticism in action. One analogy is that, while mysticism is akin to making love to the Divine, sanctity is doing the Divine will in all things. Sanctity, in other words, is the effort to behave like God at all times and in all places. Another useful analogy is that the mystic wants the joy of a live-in relationship; the saint wants the hard work of marriage.

The saint is loving in the face of evil, kind to those who express hate, completely detached from wealth and worldly power, and compassionate to those who are "unspiritual." The saint tirelessly serves others, reaches out to the homeless and the hungry and the underprivileged, and puts the needs of others ahead of himself or herself. When you exist and act in these ways, you manifest Divine love — and very little is more effective in transcending the limits of the ego.

The Dark Night of the Soul

For many, a period of deep and profound depression is necessary for deconstructing the ego. This bleak time of despair

— and ultimately, this time of transformation — has been experienced by so many mystics and saints throughout history that it has come to be known as "the dark night of the soul." This phrase comes from a poem and commentary by the same name written by Saint John of the Cross in the sixteenth century. It is another name for the purgative phase of the mystical journey.

Spiritual seekers experience the dark night of the soul in different ways and at different times in their journeys, but there are a number of common features. The person deep in the throes of this experience feels as if God has rejected or deserted him or her, and this may not only intensify the depression but also lead to a crisis of faith. The resulting despondency is eventually seen to be a sacred gift, because it purifies both mind and heart as it reveals the connecting channel to one's Divine nature and how deeply one desires it. Consequently, what seems at first to be a rejection becomes a period of intense purification: you surrender your will and allow the Divine, like a doctor operating on a patient, to lovingly extract all that is old and extraneous in preparation for the fullness of an authentic relationship.

The East-West guru Graham Ledgerwood describes the dark night of the soul this way: "The dark night occurs after considerable advancement toward higher consciousness. Indeed, the dark night usually occurs like an initiation before one of these special seekers is admitted into regular relationship with higher consciousness."[5]

My own dark night of the soul came after about a year and a half of spiritual progress. I had formally gone through the canonical procedure of progressing through the aspirant, postulant, and novice roles and was officially a Benedictine monk. But suddenly nothing seemed to "work" anymore, and I entered a period of aridity and infertility. A great emptiness filled my soul. It did not matter what sort of practices I undertook; there was simply this dry, spiritual aridity that was never moistened. I even reached a point when I did not want to meditate, pray, or chant because these practices no longer produced any "results." My spiritual ego had previously swollen with pride, and now it judged itself viciously. All that I had worked for had evaporated; I was left with nothing but spiritual barrenness and impotence.

I emerged from my dark night in stages, as if I were climbing out of a deep hole. At each step of the way, something happened to catalyze an inner shift that left me better able to make the final breakthrough. The process began when I had the opportunity to travel with Bede Griffiths and be constantly at his side for more than a week.

The administrator of the ashram asked if I would be willing to accompany Bede to an interreligious conference in the city of my birth, where the Dalai Lama and a host of other dignitaries from around the world were going to discuss spirituality together for a week. I readily accepted, excited about the opportunity to encounter so many spiritual luminaries in such an intimate setting and perhaps revive my inner life.

We set out by a specially arranged taxicab and stopped on the way for a cup of tea at a local tea stall. The eyes of the patrons popped as they watched Bede enter the tiny space, which was blackened by soot from the kitchen and littered with garbage. A group of children gathered outside to watch this English sahib dressed as a Hindu holy man drink his tea from a tall dirty glass. Bede was oblivious of the attention he was attracting, or maybe he was ignoring it,

but he was very present to people at the same time, smiling
and greeting them in a personal way whenever there was
eye contact. For my part, I was reeling from the amount of
energy moving around and through us for those few short
minutes.

On our way back to the car, a beggar approached us for
alms. Bede put his hand into his small suede purse and
pulled out a rupee coin. The beggar was surprised and, in
typical Indian beggar fashion, was about to demand more,
when his eyes connected with Bede's. Without accepting
the coin, the man fell down at his feet and prostrated right
in the middle of the street, holding up traffic. There was a
cacophonous sound of horns, and people hung out of bus
windows to catch a glimpse of this white man in saffron
robes blessing a beggar in the middle of a busy intersection.
It was like a religious ceremony, and I could not help feeling that I was with someone extraordinary.

The conference was held at the Madras Christian College, a Protestant establishment, and we settled quickly into
the room that we were about to share for the week, what
with having hardly anything to unpack. Each of us carried
a cloth bag with one spare set of unstitched monastic clothing. That evening I met many spiritual dignitaries from
around the world, but the most precious experience of all
was the private time I had with Bede, especially meditating
with him twice a day.

We had meditated together at the ashram on numerous
occasions, but then I had been absorbed in the techniques I
was practicing. Now, just about all I could do was to watch
this holy man meditate. Bede would sit on a chair, his spine
straight and his hands placed on his thighs. Then slowly, as
the meditation period unfolded, his palms would join and

his body would begin to lean forward, as though it were responding to an unseen touch of some kind. There was a distinctive change in the atmosphere when this happened.

Day after day, I witnessed this encounter, until finally I asked Bede about it. "What happens during your meditation?" I asked. "What technique do you use?" He explained that he used the full form of the Jesus prayer, in English, during meditation. Then he explained that his primary spiritual practice — not only during meditation but also throughout the day — was "the practice of the presence of God." I asked him how I could learn this method, and in reply Bede recommended a book with precisely the same title, *The Practice of the Presence of God*.

I continued to meditate with him each day, but could not help spending most of the time observing him. There was something more than mere technique happening here — which was evident from the loss of formal meditation posture — and the best way I can describe it is to compare it to a lover responding to the touch of his or her beloved. Bede was making contact with something during his meditation, and more important, that something was simultaneously reaching out to him. In hindsight, I think the experience of being with Bede while he meditated touched something deep inside me that was beyond the ability of my conscious mind to understand, and this prepared me for what was to follow.

The Practice of the Presence of God

When we returned to the ashram, I picked up a copy of *The Practice of the Presence of God* from the ashram library and began to read it with great interest. Brother Lawrence, the author of the book, was born Nicholas Herman around

1610 in Herimenil, Lorraine, a duchy of France. He fought as a young solider in the Thirty Years' War, during which he sustained a near-fatal injury to his spinal cord. The injury left him crippled and in chronic pain for the rest of his life. From an early age, he had been drawn to the spiritual life, and so after the war he dedicated himself to God, first spending a period of time in the wilderness living like one of the early desert mystics, and then entering a newly established monastery in Paris.

In times as troubled as today's, Brother Lawrence discovered, and then followed, a pure and uncomplicated way to live continually in God's presence. In *The Practice of the Presence of God*, through letters and conversations, he simply and beautifully explains how to continually walk and commune with God, not from the head but from the heart. Brother Lawrence emphasized that all physical and mental disciplines and exercises were useless unless they enabled one to arrive at union with God by means of love.

Brother Lawrence felt it was a great delusion to think that the times of prayer ought to differ from other times. When the appointed times of prayer were past, he found no difference, because he still continued talking with God, praising and thanking him with all his might. His life was a continual joy.[6] From his letters, we hear about his technique in his own words:

> I worshipped Him the oftenest I could, keeping my mind on His holy presence and recalling it as often as I found it wandered from Him. I made this my business not only at the appointed times of prayer but all the time; every hour, every minute, even in the height of my work. I drove from my

mind everything that interrupted my thoughts of
God. Over time, by often repeating these acts, they
become habitual, and the presence of God becomes
quite natural to us. I have ceased all forms of devotion and set prayers except those which my [mysti-
cal] state requires. I make it my priority to persevere
in His holy presence, wherein I maintain a simple
attention and a fond regard for God, which I may
call an actual presence of God.

My most usual method is this simple attention,
an affectionate regard for God to whom I find
myself often attached with greater sweetness and
delight than that of an infant at the mother's breast.
To choose an expression, I would call this [spiri-
tual] state the bosom of God for the inexpressible
sweetness which I taste and experience there. If, at
any time, my thoughts wander from this state from
necessity or infirmity, I am presently recalled by
inward emotions so charming and delicious that I
cannot find words to describe them.

As you can imagine, these words struck deep. I was
profoundly moved by the intimacy with the Divine that
Brother Lawrence had cultivated, and I realized what was
missing in my own spiritual life. Zealous for spiritual experiences and spiritual awakening, I had neglected the most
important reason I had come to the monastery: I had come
in response to the call of the Beloved. Excessively preoccupied with various kinds of meditation techniques, I had
forgotten the very essence of the spiritual life, which, from
the point of view of Christianity, is all about being in a
living relationship with Spirit. I do not mean to say that in

my Yoga and meditation practices I had been isolated from a sense of God, but simply that my immersion in these disciplines did not allow me to include the Divinity as a person and to live in dynamic relationship with this personhood. Even though I had attended the eucharistic celebrations each day and prayed many personal prayers, such as the Our Father and the Hail Mary, there were certain underlying mechanisms that placed the emphasis on skill and the perfection of technique. The position of the body, modulation of the breath, clarity of mind, identifying with awareness rather than the content of the mind — these had taken primary importance.

Engrossed in learning to control mind, breath, and body, I had forgotten to seek the Divine as a person, as a being whom I could interact with and, perhaps more important, who could interact with me. Like Herman Hesse's Siddhartha, I had learned to fast, to sit still in meditation for long periods, and to think deeply, and I had had many profound spiritual realizations, including ones concerning the void of Buddhism, the Self of Hinduism, and the primal energy force of kundalini. However, I had not known God as a being I could actually see, sense, and feel. Like Siddhartha, I felt that I had tried everything but still felt unfulfilled, except now I knew why: the mystery of God was not truly alive within the field of my consciousness.

Therefore, taking a copy of *The Practice of the Presence of God* and nothing else, I went to live in deep solitude about a kilometer away from the ashram, in some rice fields owned by the community. In the midst of these fields stood a solitary hermitage constructed by Father Bede himself so that he could find radical simplicity when he needed it — an impressive option, considering that his own living quarters were so sparse. The hermitage, with earth as its floor, was about fifteen square feet and fashioned entirely out of mud; the walls were just three feet high. Bamboo poles emerged from the mud walls to support a flimsy roof made from dried coconut palms, and more of the same covered three sides. The front section was uncovered, so I hung up a rag for privacy. The only furniture was an old jute cot, a bare-bones contraption of gnarled rope scantily crisscrossing a wood frame. It was all radically simple, even by Indian standards.

The hermitage faced the holy river Cauvery, in whose sacred waters millions of saints, pilgrims, and mystics had immersed their bodies. To the left, a dense mango grove extended into the neighboring property for almost half a kilometer. To the right, a coconut grove mitigated the heat of the harsh noonday sun. Additionally, the eucalyptus forest along the riverbank provided ample privacy from anyone engaged in activity along the river, which was for the most part deserted, except for the occasional goatherd or cowherd who would come by to graze and wash his animals. Fortunately, the season did not demand much activity in the rice fields, so the silence was deep.

Once a day, at lunchtime, someone delivered my main meal. I put aside some milk and fruit for the night but fasted each morning. From the time I woke up to the time I went to sleep each night, I tried to put into practice the teachings of Brother Lawrence. In whatever I looked at — the sky, the trees, the earth, the river — I tried to sense the presence of God and the grandeur of God, the entity who had fashioned these amazing creations and who was present in them in some way. I conversed with the Divine presence throughout the day and whenever I was aware at night.

To be honest with you, I did not feel much in my

practice. In fact, there was an utter emptiness to the whole process. Much of what I had previously experienced through Yoga and meditation practices was far more powerful than what I was experiencing through practicing the presence of God. Clearly, my dark night was still unfolding. But something was happening beyond the level of my awareness.

With great determination, I brought to my practice all the intensity of my desire to know God. Hour after hour, day after day, week after week, I practiced, as best I could, putting all my heart and soul into the process, even though I did not feel the joys or spiritual consolations that Brother Lawrence describes. I had read Saint John of the Cross and Saint Teresa of Avila and knew of the personal relationship that these great mystics had had with God, and I was acutely aware that I did not know the Divine in their way. I knew also of Mira Bai, the Indian princess and mystic who was a great devotee of Lord Krishna and who sensed his presence everywhere, and of Ramakrishna, who passionately loved the goddess Kali and saw her in everything. Their experience too was intimate and alive. Still, I persisted in my practice, even extending my retreat by a couple of weeks, waiting, seeking, longing — but there was nothing more than my ego, the hermitage, and my practice. My dark night only got darker.

One evening, as the crows came to roost in the mango trees, I left the hermitage, frustrated and disappointed. The sun was beginning to set as I walked barefoot to the ashram and sat down dejectedly underneath a large tree near the temple gateway. The bell rang for evening prayer, and I took my seat among the monks. That evening, the reading from the Old Testament was about Moses's encounter with God.

These verses raised a question in my mind: What would it be like to see the face of God, to look directly into those Divine eyes, or to hear his or her or its voice, however it would come through to me? It struck me that Moses did not practice any form of Yoga or meditation, but something had approached him, without his even asking for it, and "it" had communicated itself to him. I realized then that I wanted to know God as God was.

So I went to my hut, the one I had left behind when I went into solitude, the same one that overlooked the field of elephant grass where I had had my out-of-body experience, and I closed the door. I sat in the lotus position on my bed, which consisted of nothing more than a raised wooden plank about eight inches off the ground, and I asked God to reveal himself to me. I begged, pleaded, pestered, implored, badgered, beseeched, harassed, entreated, wheedled, nagged, cajoled, coaxed, enticed, and used every psychological trick in the book to convince God that I wanted to see him, face-to-face, just once.

The Day My Heart Exploded

I have no idea how long I did this, but at some point I dropped off to sleep. In the morning, I awoke to find myself in a posture known as *yoga mudra*, legs folded in the lotus posture and head touching the ground. It was excruciatingly painful getting out of the posture, for my legs had gone to sleep. The angelus bell rang, and I ignored the call to prayer: I was upset with God. Slowly, I made my way to the bathroom, about fifty feet from my hut. As I brushed my teeth at the faucet inside, I could feel some energy building up on the floor of the bathroom. I had, of course, experienced similar energy before, except this time I could feel it extend across the entire floor of the bathroom, as though water were rising slowly, seeping up from the floor onto my bare feet and into the room. The energy continued to rise, slowly and steadily. I could feel it in my ankles, rising up into my shins and my knees. At the same time, I could feel it rise in the whole bathroom, as though it were being occupied by some sort of presence. I felt uneasy and stepped outside.

There, at the faucet located outside, I tried to finish my brushing. In that moment I realized that the entire grounds of the ashram were filled with this energy. The trees, the stones, the hermitages, the water running from the faucet, the clothes-washing stone beside it — everything was throbbing with energy. I looked at the field of elephant grass and at the eucalyptus forest and the river beyond. All of it was pulsating with the same energy. I looked up at the sky and the clouds, and there too the energy extended its influence, vibrating and shimmering in the dull glow of the predawn sun.

Walking quickly to the temple, I settled down in front of the tabernacle with my toothbrush at my side, the paste still damp on the bristles. My experience inside the temple was equally terrifying: the walls of the temple were not solid any longer; they were liquidlike and glowing with energy. The stone tabernacle was like a simmering cauldron, pulsating and throbbing as if it might explode at any moment. Bede arrived and began chanting the mantra "Om namah Christaaya." Shortly after, others joined in, and it seemed as if the doors of the tabernacle had been flung wide open and huge shafts of luminous energy were bursting out, hitting me smack in my heart space. I was emotionally paralyzed and greatly frightened. Not wanting to continue in that environment, I got up and made my way to Bede's hermitage, more out of instinct than by plan.

When I arrived at his hermitage, I was struck by the intensity of energy there, especially on the front porch where he meditated each day. This was a beautiful spot overlooking a grove of coconut trees whose frond arrangement formed a beautiful concave shape. The moment I looked at the sky, a massive force like a clap of thunder came hurtling through that concave space, as though it were a portal to another realm, pushing me against the wall of Bede's hermitage, hard against the ochre brick. This is exactly how Bede found me when he arrived from chanting the *namajapa*.

Without much ado, he took me into his hut and sat me down on his bed. Pulling up the only chair in the room, he took my hands and waited patiently for me to tell him what was going on. I could not speak, so I gestured that I would like to write. He pulled his Bible from the shelf and opened to the blank insert behind the front cover. It was interesting that he chose this book, rather than a scrap of paper from his wastepaper basket. "I am overwhelmed!" I wrote. He smiled and nodded. He knew exactly what was happening. We sat that way for the entire hour of meditation. Tears continually rolled down my cheeks. "I have to go to Mass," he said finally. "You stay here and wait for me."

I sat there in his hermitage, terrified, hugging myself, not knowing what to do. All of a sudden, the Jesus prayer began to say itself inside me, in English. I had not used this form for more than a year, ever since I had started using Sanskrit. I had no control of my mind or my heart or my body. Everywhere I turned, whether I kept my eyes closed or open, I could sense this energy, but it wasn't just energy; there was an Otherness about it too, a "beingness" that was definitely not human. Whatever it was, it was intent on communicating with me, and I could feel that intention by means of something within the energy that was pushing, almost forcing itself onto me.

Bede returned, and I tried to explain what was going on, but I couldn't. The moment I tried to speak, I would choke, because I needed to use language to describe the experience, and the experience was everywhere, even in the words I wanted to use and in the muscles I needed to use to say them. Later, after I left his hermitage and tried to move around the ashram and go about my day as usual, I found that I could not function properly, because I wept profusely. I could not socialize either, because the most frightening part of all was the amount of energy that came pouring out of the eyes of the human beings and animals I encountered on the property. Whenever I glanced at a person's eyes, I would see only two glowing orbs of gold suffused with energy as bright as sunlight, streaming out into my own. I was blinded by the glare and needed to look away. Even more terrifying were the eyes of children. The energy that came through their eyes was magnified ten times over. It was a Sunday morning when this happened, so children from the village had come to the ashram along with their parents to attend Mass, after which they played about the ashram. I was overwhelmed with the immensity of the light and the throbbing energy that was everywhere.

Bede suggested that I return to the hermitage in the paddy fields so that I did not have to encounter people. The English form of the Jesus prayer continued to say itself in me day and night. I hardly slept or ate during this period, though the food continued to be delivered faithfully each afternoon. The entire experience pulsated throughout the day and night too, and I was always wide awake. The mantra just said itself in me over and over again, whether I was awake or asleep, even during my dreams. Part of me was witnessing and another part was experiencing, and both were functioning at peak levels. The experience lasted many weeks, and it was almost a full month before I could return to the ashram and continue with my life there. Even then, I still could not speak of the experience. The moment I tried to speak of it, the intensity would return with such force that I would instantly choke, both emotionally and verbally. Slowly, I resumed my practice of Hatha Yoga and meditation, which helped me recover my balance, particularly the yoga postures and breathing techniques I had learned. It was several months before any sense of normalcy returned. Something had shifted deep within me, and I continued to feel the effects, like the aftermath of a psychic earthquake or tsunami.

Spiritual Intimacy

The dark night of the soul teaches you, as it taught me, that you cannot just "get God" or "know Spirit" or "become enlightened" as though such an experience were a thing, an object. I love the Buddhist statement "If you meet the Buddha on the road, kill him." This powerful lesson implies that we need to watch out for projections, creations of the mind that substitute for reality, especially spiritual realities. Authentic spiritual experiences are hard to objectify, as they are powerfully subjective, although they do engender a certain level of objective awareness.

If God or Spirit is alive and conscious and contains within itself some semblance of personhood (from which we, as humans, derive our own sense of personhood), there has to be the possibility of mutual, reciprocal love, of love flowing from both sides, human as well as Divine. This means that it or she or he has the power to reject you or love you, to interact consciously with you.

In other words, you cannot make the Divine love you: you cannot force the relationship as an act of will. You may use your will to choose to pursue the relationship, but to actually know God, to consummate the relationship, you must surrender your will entirely and allow God to choose you. Father Keating explains: "The work of the will in prayer is real work, but it is one of receiving. Receiving is one of the most difficult kinds of activity there is. To receive God is the chief work in contemplative prayer."[7]

This is why I feel that the relationship we cultivate and then build with the Divine is very much like a marriage. Why marriage? Why not conversation or dialogue or partnership? Because only marriage, as a metaphor, carries all the meanings that must characterize an authentic relationship with the Divine. Marriage is a sacred partnership of equals, a special kind of relationship that involves intimacy as well as hard work, shared vision as well as the honoring of individuality, and mutual support as well as challenge. In the spiritual fire of marriage, we are challenged constantly to work through our shadow sides, dismantle our false selves, and progress toward wholeness and integrity, because our marriage partners mirror our gradual transformations and regressions, and we are engaged in this mirroring process all the time. Most important, we cannot take marriage for granted. We must be willing to work at continually nurturing it, or it simply falls apart. It is precisely for this reason that Christian monks, nuns, and priests consider themselves "married to Christ."

Another important feature of marriage is that it is a relationship in which we retain our differences and our uniqueness while, at the same time, realizing that our partnership is greater than either individual. Marriage offers an engaged partnership and a sense of equality, which is the direction in which our religions must head. In marriage, however much we may dislike certain aspects of the other, we are committed to growth in love for this person. Love is always patient, kind, and forgiving. Yet love also challenges us to grow.

In a marriage between human beings, one of the most important qualities is trust. Similarly, it takes trust to stay engaged in your relationship with the spiritual dimension of your being. Many spiritual seekers move from practice to practice, teacher to teacher, system to system, because the novelty of the approach quickly wears off. It takes trust to repeatedly turn within and passionately seek the Beloved in the depths of your being. The process mirrors human relationships. At first, you are excited about a person as you glimpse the radiance of his or her soul. Then, as you begin to engage in a relationship, the structures of the person's ego begin to show, just as your own ego structures do. It is trust that keeps you working through the difficulties that ensue.

All relationships take work, and your relationship with the Divine is no different, except that the Divine has no ego. The Spirit is pure, undivided consciousness, and you have to discover that a part of you is spirit too, existing in the image and likeness of the Divine. One danger of the New Age movement, in its indiscriminate obsession for all kinds of spiritual experience, is the tendency to want to sleep with the Divine (meaning, to have intimacy with God) while avoiding the hard work of true relationship.

Again, this mentality is not too far from what we see in the realm of human relationships.

In a good human marriage, love infuses the partnership and becomes the underlying reason for everything the two partners do to build and deepen the relationship. Fidelity, trust, intimacy, and self-sacrifice must all flow from this love, not from fear, coercion, or even a sense of duty or responsibility. Doing good or being good out of fear of going to hell, for example, is a very limited expression of charity. To love for love's sake, on the other hand, is the most natural thing in the world. It is not self-seeking, does not have a why, and contains no hidden agenda. To learn to live and love without a why is the most liberating human experience.

It is the same in our relationship with the Divine. Practicing spirituality out of fear or duty (conditions that affect Hindus as well as Christians) stifles the love at the core of the relationship. Practicing to get ahead in the game — to "advance," as it is sometimes called in spiritual circles — is equally misguided, because it only builds the ego. When spiritual practice is excessively goal oriented, we lose touch with the energy of soul, which is process oriented, and the ego inevitably contaminates the effort.

One should also guard against duty or obligation to spiritual teachers. While such duty and obligation can initially push us beyond our apathy or self-centeredness, it is still very limiting. A good spiritual teacher always inspires spiritual discipline that stems from love, rather than duty, fear, or a grandiose vision of spiritual advancement.

IN YOUR SPIRITUAL JOURNEY, it is helpful to give some consideration to how you want to live your life should you be fortunate enough to have the Divine come into your heart as your constant companion. If you are given this ultimate gift of Divine grace, how are you going to make sense of it and use it for the good of the world?

Not everyone has the inclination to live continually in the highest experience of the Divine, even though every person may be fully capable of doing so. It takes a remarkable being to choose the Divine above all else and remain satisfied with such a choice for the entire period of his or her life. Such figures have graced our planet throughout the course of human history, and they continue to shine as beacons of light for the rest of us. Ramana Maharshi, Ramakrishna, Saint Teresa of Avila, and Saint Francis of Assisi are a few examples. I place my mentor, Bede Griffiths, in this category as well.

Samadhi, in the Yoga tradition, is the supreme state of enlightenment, or God realization. Living in Samadhi is a choice, but it is a mutually reciprocated choice. When we choose the Divine above all else, the Divine returns the gesture. All the great mystics have demonstrated this level of connectedness, which manifests itself as in the uninterrupted holiness I saw in Bede Griffiths.

I was given a powerful experience of the Divine, almost a revelation. And yet, in the end, I chose not to live fulltime in Samadhi. There were many reasons for this choice, and the circumstances surrounding it were complex, but ultimately I made the choice because, as I can see in retrospect, I lacked the maturity to handle it. I desired the experience and was granted it, but, in Hindu terms, karmic impressions of previously crystallized ego structures remained to be worked through. I have been working through these structures ever since that experience.

Even though I chose not to live the life of a formal holy

man in constant connection with the Divine while completely renouncing all else, I did not renounce the gift that I had been given. The glimpse of ultimate reality that I had been honored with transformed me completely, giving me a new perspective on the many games and layers of the ego. Zen has an insightful analogy that illustrates the process. At first, the river is a river, the tree a tree. This is one's typical learned perception, gained through our conventional education in the world. Next, the river is not a river and the tree is not a tree, because you no longer take the outward form for granted and you put all your observations under the scrutiny of spiritual discipline. Like a scientist observing water or tree bark under a microscope, you get a glimpse into the inner structure and hidden workings of the universe. Finally, the river is a river once again and a tree is a tree once again, except now you are experiencing both river and tree through new eyes and transformed vision.

6

Yoga and the Revitalization
of Christianity

THERE IS A LEGEND IN INDIA about the famous Indian mystic Kabir, whose poems have been made popular in the United States by the American poet Robert Bly. When Kabir died, Muslims and Hindus, both wanting to claim him as their own saint, were quarreling over his dead body. The former wanted it buried, the latter cremated. The problem was divinely resolved when someone asked the two groups to lift the sheet covering the body, and all that remained was a pile of flower petals!

Saint Paul preached that "in Christ" there is neither Jew nor Gentile, yet every major spiritual tradition in the world has used division to deliver its message. Christianity has separated the world into the saved and the damned. Muslims have a similar concept, dividing the world into believers and nonbelievers. Jews divide humanity into the chosen and the rejected. Buddhists divide the world between the enlightened and the nonenlightened, and Hindus discriminate between those who are liberated and those caught in the web of illusory reality, maya. Yet we are all held together in existence by the same principle of life, the same Divine source who is patiently loving and nurturing us, moment after moment. The common understanding that unites all traditions is that we can either exist in a fallen state, asleep and ignorant, or wake up, become conscious, and restore our connection to the greater whole.

A few Christmases ago, I was part of an interspiritual conference at the Sivananda Yoga Retreat in the Bahamas, where I attended a workshop presented by ninety-year-old Rabbi Joseph Gelberman of New York City. In the workshop, I was profoundly moved by Gelberman, who combines the Yogic tradition with Hebrew mantras in exercises known as "Kabbala in Motion." He taught that God deliberately did not give the whole truth to any one tradition, because that was the only way to ensure that the adherents of all of them would work together. For any tradition to claim that it has the whole truth is an insult to God. Gelberman uses the Jewish menorah to symbolize commonality: each candle burns in a stem rooted in a common cast. Bede used a similar analogy: the great religions are like the five fingers of a hand — they all meet at the palm, and they work together in any action.

If Christianity is to seek an alliance with the Yoga tradition, with the intention of working together for the peace and spiritual welfare of the world, then it must first understand and appreciate the power of Yoga and the value it contributes to Western society and the world today. The reasons for the growing popularity of Yoga are manifold, the most prominent reason being its powerful and practical spiritual processes. Of special importance is the fact that these processes rely on experience rather than on faith or belief. Yoga's results can be tested and tasted firsthand, and quickly too. But there are two problems with this. The first is that this, unfortunately, becomes ammunition for Christian fundamentalists who decry the practicality of the Yogic system as being antithetical to faith, while in reality it should be considered complementary, since Yoga offers a direct experience of God that can and does support Christianity and other types of faith. The second problem is that Yoga practitioners can become complacent, even proud and arrogant, believing that they are in absolute control of their spiritual life and experience. This can also cause them to look down on people of faith, particularly practicing Christians. If Christianity is to take the first steps in building a relationship with Yoga, what will they be? Latin Christianity and evangelical Christianity have placed the emphasis on salvation through the profession of faith in Jesus Christ as Lord and Savior, rather than on the transformational teaching of Jesus. While this works for Christians born into the tradition, practitioners of experiential spiritual traditions such as Yoga find it a barrier to their appreciation of Christianity. If, however, Christianity can shift the emphasis of its mission to explain that the spiritual growth and challenges resulting from the essential teachings of Jesus are fundamental, and then allow profession of faith to be an option for those who naturally come to it on their own, this will make an enormous difference in Christianity's relationship with other religions, particularly wisdom-based Eastern religions. Jesus himself declared, "Not everyone who says Lord, Lord, will come to me, but only those who do the will of my Father" (Matthew 7:21). Of course it is possible to profess faith in Jesus as a personal savior and call oneself a Christian but not follow the teaching of Jesus. Conversely, it is possible to follow the teaching of Jesus without calling oneself a Christian and without believing in him as a personal savior or as the only way to God. So who is the real Christian here? This curious situation is rather unique to Christianity and rarely if ever encountered in any other tradition. However, a comparable condition exists in Yoga, as I will soon point out.

Christianity's Interspiritual Hurdles

What are some of the biggest hurdles Christianity must overcome in order to relate to Yoga and Eastern traditions in general? Apart from the opening salvo "Do you accept Jesus as your Lord and Savior?" the following are the top three hurdles. The first is Christianity's view of the body, especially in terms of human sexuality. The role of the body in spiritual practice needs to be redefined, and the power of human sexuality as an inherent spiritual possibility must be acknowledged.

Next, Christianity must start paying attention to the relationship between food and consciousness. Christians need to understand that what we put into our bodies does indeed have an effect upon our spiritual life and practice.

Then, there is the militant and negative language of Christianity, with its concepts of the anti-Christ, the devil, and eternal punishment; the constant emphasis on sinfulness; the threat of burning in hell; and so on. Christianity has to rethink its message in terms of pro-life language and present itself in terms that are more positive.

The problem, though, for those who are tired of and disillusioned with Christianity, is throwing the baby out with the bathwater. Is *everything* in Christianity unworthy of our acceptance? Unfortunately, one of the most common attitudes adopted by Yoga practitioners in America is that, yes, it is. Interestingly, most of them come from Christian or Jewish backgrounds; and Christians, in particular, do not know how to reconcile their Christian energies with their Yogic lifestyles, although they would like to if only it were possible to do so in a meaningful way. In the past, Christianity took the stance that it was the only true tradition.[1] All others were false or, at best, lesser. It is crucial that the Yoga community in the West not repeat this error by comparing the positive aspects of Yoga with the negative tendencies of Christianity.

Regretfully, there is a prevailing trend among Western Yoga practitioners to look down on Christianity without bothering to truly understand it. Jacob Needleman, in his brilliant work *The American Soul*, says, "Murder and bloody war under the banner of Christian love; devastation under the banner of submission to Allah — such examples abound in human history. To be disillusioned with Christianity because of the Inquisition or the Crusades, or their less vivid counterparts in modern life, does not necessarily represent a judgment on the Christian teaching itself, but on how broken pieces of it had combined and been used in the course of human history. This has been the fate of most of the great religions of the world."[2]

Christianity's Interspiritual Contributions

What are some of the ways that the Yoga tradition can benefit from Christianity? In my experience of Yoga teachers and practitioners around the United States, I have not found most of them to be exceptionally enlightened or significantly more spiritual than Christian practitioners. In fact, if you take out the part about Jesus being the only Son of God and the only way to salvation, you will find that a good many practicing Christians do have a rather solid and committed spiritual practice and that they do exercise and discipline themselves in a number of commendable ways. To be fair, it must be acknowledged that yoga teachers and practitioners have their own limitations, which they sincerely struggle with, and there are aspects of Christianity that can be valuable to them, particularly the essential Christian teaching that God is love, and that this love of God is a gift, not the result of spiritual effort.[3] There is also the sense in Christianity and Judaism that God is actually seeking us out in a personal way. The East concentrates on the human search for the Divine, and, while this is an intense and commendable process, it inculcates a sense of utter self-reliance that can miss the principle of grace. Grace, in the words of Caroline Myss, is "unmerited divine assistance coming to us directly from God to help regenerate our spirits and our lives."[4] As a result, while Yogis may know intellectually that God is love, within Christianity there is a palpable sense of love by grace, a love that transcends karma and reaches out despite it, and this can offer a refreshing balance to, even respite from, the emphasis on effort characteristic of the East. Indeed, it is an extraordinary blessing to experience this sense of being loved so deeply and unconditionally by the Divine and in such a palpable manner, and this is Christianity's gift. And there is a certain loneliness and isolation in the Yogic way that can be mitigated by this love.

We must keep in mind that these are generalizations, and that one can see this sense of love being infused in Western Yoga through the practice of *kirtan*, or devotional singing. However, there are standards of Christian love that can be incorporated into Yoga practice, just as there are standards concerning mystical depth in Yoga practice that can be incorporated into Christian spirituality. While a certain emphasis may help a tradition focus on, develop, and even specialize in a specific spiritual aspect, other equally important aspects can remain undernourished in the tradition as a whole, although individuals, groups, and sects may address these undernourished aspects. For instance, in Christianity, love has developed powerfully in the social dimension, evidenced by helping others, especially the poor and marginalized. Expressions of this type are not absent from Hinduism, but this type of love is not as well developed. The East can learn more about it from Christianity — that is, one spiritual tradition can be inspired by and grow within itself a standard of love developed by another. Similarly, Yoga has developed powerful ways to foster concentration, a standard that can be categorized as a means of loving God, one that allows us to reach out to God internally, with minimal distractions from the mind, body, and emotions. Christianity has its own means of concentration but can learn much from Yoga. The idea that Yogis are experts at concentration is a generalization, just as it is a generalization to say that Christians are supposed to exemplify love or Buddhists compassion. There are always groups and individuals who fall short of this ideal, but they are not representative of the large numbers of individuals within those traditions who do exemplify the ideal in their lives and actions.

Perhaps because American and Canadian practitioners of Yoga come from Christian and Jewish backgrounds, the standards of love that are prevalent in Western culture, and that result from the good influence of Christianity, have already been incorporated into Western Yoga practice. I assume the same is true in Europe and Australia; I am not in a position to determine this, however, since I rarely go there. What I am driving at is that the practice of love is a Yoga in itself, and that Christians are arguably the masters of it, or so they should be. Whether or not individual members display this does not matter; the point is to identify what the tradition upholds as its central teaching.

When Jesus asked his disciples to "love the Lord your God with all your heart and soul and love your neighbor as yourself" (Mark 12:30–31), he implied that this love of neighbor is to extend to everyone, especially the marginalized of society, whom Jesus cared about greatly and wanted his disciples to as well. He asked that they go the extra mile, turn the other cheek, give cloak as well as shirt. He also wanted his followers to reach out and feed the hungry, clothe those who needed to be clothed, visit the sick and the imprisoned, and care for the widow and orphan. In other words, he wanted his followers to attend to more than just what was in front of them. These are explicit, perhaps benchmark, standards of love that every Yogi can aspire to.

In Yoga practice, this is often referred to as the practice of selfless service or "Karma Yoga," the Yoga of selfless action, and there are Yoga practitioners, teachers, and organizations that truly engage in selfless action. However, for the most part, Yoga studios and teachers offer Karma Yoga as something students do within the confines of their organization, such as cleaning the grounds or chopping vegetables. The essential Christian teaching about love requires more: the willingness to inconvenience oneself, even to deprive oneself, for the sake of love, and the willingness to go outside one's normal range to do so. This is lofty Yoga, indeed, and many Christians, even if they do not fully embody such standards, unconsciously aspire to them be-cause doing so is an essential teaching of Christian Yoga. But some parts of this teaching can be impractical, espe-cially if practiced out of sentimentality. This is why the discernment discussed earlier is so important, as Jesus im-plied when he asked his disciples to be "as wise as serpents as well as gentle as doves" (Matthew 10:16).

Christianity also teaches that there is a way to reach out with love to the Divine that is beyond the scope of tech-nique, a way of becoming like a child in the Divine presence that is accompanied by an indelible sense of Divine love. It is a matter of learning to become available to God or Spirit as an act of loving intention. Catholics practice this act of becoming available to God or Spirit as a form of meditation in front of the Blessed Sacrament. It is known as adoration: simply being present to the presence of God without want-ing anything, not even spiritual experiences. There are In-dian Yogis who demonstrate an ability to do this, and it is common among Hindus, who often become absorbed in silent communion in temples as well as in their homes. However, this kind of unconditional quietude is difficult for the average Western Yogi, who is an effort-oriented and goal-oriented practitioner. It would, as a result, be good for Yogis, Western Yogis in particular, to develop unconditional loving attentiveness and interior divine adoration in com-bination with a passionate love for the poor and the mar-ginalized that expresses itself in loving action in the world. In other words, the experience of love and the cultivation of it as a Yogi should be included in some way in the formal teaching and practice of Yoga.

In India, this sense of love, especially in its external expressions, has traditionally been absent in Yoga, essentially because of the general emphasis on effort and technique together with the emphasis on detachment and interior absorption. There is of course the devotional Yoga tradition, an exception to the classic Yoga tradition, which does not overtly advocate cultivation of the experience of love. We might say that the Yoga of Christianity is precisely this: the cultivation of love, the "effort" to love, the mystical experience of ultimate love and lovingness.

The ultimate goal of Yoga, at least as described by Patanjali's famous Yoga Sutras, is Samadhi, which is absorption in the divine energy or beingness of God as pure consciousness through knowing the true Self. However, we need to realize that just as in Christianity one may profess faith in Jesus as Savior but not follow his teachings, in Yoga one may tap into the nature of God without having a relationship with God. In other words, we may control the mind and emotions so that we glimpse the nature of God, but in the process, one may relinquish what is perhaps the most valuable of human possibilities: a dynamic and reciprocal relationship with the divine. Additionally, even though advanced states of Yoga may avert the tendency to confuse altered mental states with divine states of consciousness, there is an imminent danger in the early stages that an inexperienced Yoga practitioner may confuse ultimate states of consciousness with self-absorbed awareness. Christianity offers a sense of Otherness that can be a healthy balance when one is cultivating a relationship with ultimate reality in which oneness comes about through mutual reciprocity.

Christianity and Judaism, can, I believe, offer a strong foundation in other-centeredness that a Yoga practitioner can benefit from in the early stages of spiritual development. The Upanishads, for instance, contain some profound teachings about Yogic experience that, in individuals lacking spiritual maturity, cause more harm than good. Take the underlying ontological assumption in Hinduism "Aham Brahmasmi," which literally means, "I am God," or that my identity and God's identity are one and the same.[5] While this can be validated from a philosophical standpoint, for it is a profound mystical realization, it can be spiritually damaging to the immature spiritual seeker because it limits God to one's awareness, whatever that might be. It is dangerous when individuals assume they are God during early or even intermediate stages of the spiritual journey, which is why Christianity generally rejects this language of identification with God. However, such expressions can be found in the works of some Western mystics, as in the advanced mysticism of Meister Eckhart, who was, regrettably, silenced as a heretic. Christianity may need to revisit this sort of language in order to engage with the East and to encourage the development of the advanced mystical experience within oneself. Moreover, this engagement with the East can help lay out a framework for the inner life for advanced Christian practitioners, one that takes into consideration the chakras and Yogic states of consciousness. As noted in chapter 4, both traditions can benefit from such a dialogue with each other.

Another problem with the language of Yoga, one that has often come up in my discussions with Eastern-influenced spiritual practitioners, is a famous statement from the Bhagavad Gita, "The man [or woman] who has seen the truth thinks, 'I am not the doer'" (5:8), meaning Spirit is the sole doer in all things. This, too, has a certain ontological truth, since everything we do is ultimately done through the power of God or Spirit, but living this principle during the early or middle stages of spiritual development can foster a disassociative mentality to life and negate the power of soul we are entrusted with. For instance, to say, "I am not the doer" can encourage us to relinquish our spiritual responsibilities, abort our spiritual adulthood, and deny ourselves the power of choice that distinguishes us as ensouled beings.

Having grown up in India, and having visited the country annually for the past ten years, I recognize — and most Indians will agree with me — that we Indians, as a people, often do not take a stand for justice when it concerns others. Moreover, we all too easily distance ourselves from other people, ascribing their circumstances to fate or karma. Christianity and Judaism teach us that we have the spiritual power to intervene — and in some instances have an obligation to do so — in order to help others who are less fortunate, for by doing so we become the channel through which the Divine can act and reveal itself to the person or community that needs help. The Yoga of Jesus is to love, despite the other's ego, despite their karma, despite their ignorance, for the power of love can transform their ego and their karma and their ignorance. It may not do so immediately, as was evident from Jesus's death on the cross, but the transformation will take place eventually and will be far more powerful than any other means, for love is the ultimate tool of transformation. This exercise of human will in alignment with Divine love is an exercise of spiritual power, a Yoga if you will, for through this power we have the capacity to relinquish egotistical habits and culturally conditioned programming — or to refuse the Divine nature, presence, and will.

Christian Enlightenment

It is also necessary to explore the Christian contribution to the experience of spiritual enlightenment. What distinguishes it is its awareness of the power of one's soul to influence the communal process of enlightenment. From the deeper Christian point of view, individual choice has a role in the grand fulfillment of the universe that has been "groaning in travail" (Romans 8:22). This is why the Second Coming of Jesus is better seen as a gradual process that ushers in a new consciousness, a process that requires our consent and conscious participation. It is not understood as a dramatic appearance that, in a moment, separates the good from the bad, for that would indicate Divine impatience.

Christian enlightenment, then, is the call to actively participate in the Divine vision for humanity. The new consciousness is ushered into the world, into humanity, and into all of creation. All human beings take part in this conscious partnership with the Divine, and all support one another, as individuals and as communities. Furthermore, from the Christian point of view, the human response to this cocreated consciousness is prompted by love rather than a desire for *truth* or even knowledge of the Self. While all approaches arguably lead to the same end, each process shapes the individual and the world uniquely, and this must be appreciated, which is precisely why the Judaic and Christian viewpoints are worthy of inclusion in the yogic perspective that is, for the most part, strongly individualistic.

The Christian view of enlightenment is also unique in that it posits that enlightenment is both individual and communal. The Eastern view, on the other hand, states that it is entirely individual and pertains strictly to human consciousness, meaning that the rest of creation and other conscious individual beings are not drawn into it: they are, according to the enlightened view, an illusion. Not that they don't exist in themselves, but that, in the experience of enlightenment, the Self shines in its own being and this Self is the same Self of everything else. In other words, there are no particular or individual identities in the Self. It is somewhat difficult to wrap the mind around this, for it is an experience, not an idea. There is a huge difference between the Eastern view and the Christian and Jewish viewpoints.

For instance, when the great Indian sage Ramana Maharshi was asked about the conflict between becoming enlightened and helping others, he is supposed to have responded, "But there are no others." Here, of course, he is speaking from a profound mystical experience, a fullness of Self, not selfishness. In the Eastern view, there is only the one, indivisible Supreme Spirit residing in all things and all people, and when we awaken to its presence within us, all distinctions are illusory and simply fall away: we see only God, in ourselves and in others and in all things. There is no differentiation in this vision — only a seamless connectedness to an infinite continuum. This is similar to the Buddhist view of nirvana, in which the illusion of separateness is "snuffed out," which is the literal meaning of the word *nirvana*.

I suggest that, while recognizing the value of the Hindu and Buddhist views, we can simultaneously acknowledge and value the power of the Christian and Judaic view that there is ultimate value in the individual parts of creation and in the individual processes as well as in all of human suffering. In this view, every creative process, from the very beginning to the very end of time as we know it has ultimate value, meaning, and purpose. The various phenomena of creation are not an illusion that drops away, but are integral and intrinsic to our individual and collective enlightenment. In this view, every atomic reaction and every biological process from the beginning to the end of time is fulfilled: "For creation itself will be set free from its bondage to decay and obtain the glorious liberty of the children of Spirit" (Romans 8:21). And so, every amoeba, deer, and dinosaur has meaning and purpose and participates in the experience of a collective enlightened fulfillment, the result of the awakened consciousness that has been precipitated by conscious human participation in the divine purpose for our universe. Why can't this be concurrent with the ultimate realization of consciousness?

IN THE WEST, Yoga has become popular enough to spawn its own culture, with specific clothing lines and clichés. Yoga is big business today. One thing we must guard against in this process of cultural development and commercialization is the loss of the deepest aspects of this wonderful discipline. We must also recognize the danger that accompanies the development of a spiritual ego in Yoga practitioners who assume that, because they are spiritual practitioners, they know more about spirituality than others do, and who express this ego by denigrating Christianity. On the brighter side, Western Yoga continues to integrate more and more with Western psychology to produce a healthier form that is a prototype for the future.

I sincerely hope that a conversation begins between the Christian and the Yogi within each spiritual seeker who reads this work. We are all Yogis. Yoga is union, balance, harmony, and peace. However, our peace and our balance and our connection to our source are constantly being challenged by life's circumstances, our changing world and health, our complex relationships, and the often intricate maneuvering and meandering in our professional lives. Yoga shows us how to restore and maintain harmony by honoring our physical bodies and disciplining our minds. This Yoga is universal.

Christianity too is universal. The word *catholic* actually means "universal." Consciousness of Christ and the awakening of universal consciousness in every human being is essential to our evolution. And we must recognize that Christ consciousness is already a part of other traditions, that it is greater than Christianity. In the same way, Yogic powers, processes, and capabilities are universal and exist in other traditions. Yet, as we have seen, Christianity and Yoga both offer the individual practitioner specific gifts and specific challenges because of the emphases of their individual paths. Each Yogi, and each Christian, has to find his or her way to integrate the challenges that the other tradition presents and to embrace the gifts that each has to offer. Yogis challenge themselves physically on a regular basis, and today Yoga in the West has moved beyond that physical dimension. Many Western Yogis now challenge themselves spiritually, mentally, and morally.[6]

The Way and the Truth

For many Christians, Jesus's declaration "I am the Way, the Truth, and the Life" proves Christianity's supremacy over other traditions, which are considered to be untrue and therefore as leading to death. Bede Griffiths often joked, "Thank God, he did not say, 'I am the only Way, the only Truth, and the only Life.'" To understand what Jesus said from the inner, mystical perspective is to acknowledge the archetypal universality of the Christ Self, which can and should be compared to Atman and the true Self, as we have already done.

From the outward, social perspective, Jesus taught radical dependence on God, which he himself practiced, and which he illustrated in his directive to his disciples to "carry no purse, no bag, no sandals" (Luke 10:4–6). This too has its corresponding parallel in the Indian Yogic tradition of *sannyasa*, a complete renunciation of everything but God alone, which was already a spiritual institution in India hundreds of years before the time of Jesus and continues to the present day. As Cynthia Bourgeault points out in *The Wisdom Jesus*, Jesus did not teach in a vacuum. Capernaum, where he did most of his teaching, was located on the Silk Road, and spiritual ideas and concepts from India could very well have reached him through merchants and travelers. Contrary to some theories that Jesus went to India, it is far more conclusive that India came to Jesus.

Many Hindus have a hard time with Christians who preach the message of Jesus while living in comparable luxury, unlike their own radical monks, who seem to be following Jesus's directives far more than Christian missionaries do. For although Christian missionaries may live simply in India, their accommodations are far more luxurious than those of the Indian monk, Yogi, and frequently even the ordinary person who sleeps on the floor, eats with his or her hands, and wears pieces of unstitched clothing around the body. Only after the pioneering work of my mentor and his peers did Christian religious in India begin to adopt simple Indian clothing.

The important renunciation, though, is not the renunciation of possessions or lifestyle but the renunciation of "I" and "mine." Bede Griffiths, who lived an austere life as both Yogi and Christian monk, explained, "A sannyasi is one who is totally detached from the world and from himself. It is detachment which is the keyword. It does not matter what material possessions you have, so long as you are not attached to them. The one thing which you have to abandon unconditionally is your 'self.' If you can give up your self, your 'ego,' you can have anything you like, wife and family, houses and lands — but who is able to give up his self?"[7] Jesus captured the idea succinctly: "Those who lose their [egos] for my sake will find it [divine nature]" (Matthew 10:39). Here again, the motivation for renunciation is love. The Bhagavad Gita expounds on the same principle: "Abandoning all desires, acting without craving, free from all thoughts of 'I' and 'mine,' that [person] finds inner peace. Absorbed in this divine state, everywhere, always, even at the moment of death, such a [person] vanishes into God's bliss."[8]

Yoga and Christianity as originally taught by Jesus share a radicalism. However, in modern times both traditions — especially Western Yoga and Western Christianity — have adapted this radicalism to life in the world. Not everyone is ready for the intensity of Jesus's core teachings and practices. However, the ultimate goal of both traditions is the discovery of the absolute consciousness that Jesus called Father, and that in India is called Brahman. This search for ultimate reality can be undertaken while living a normally engaged life in the world. This "normal life" may be the healthiest and sanest form of mysticism. Christianity has a complementary objective: it asks that, while searching for the Absolute, we also make our world a better place by being kind and loving to others. However, whereas the search for divine mystery and spiritual experience has faded into the background in Christian spirituality, it is being revived today by individuals and organizations such as those that I mention in the resources section.

The practice of Yoga, together with the philosophical vision of the Upanishads, can help restore a unitive world-view to Christianity, in which it rediscovers the world penetrated by the supreme consciousness of God. This will help bring a more intimate sense of Divine presence into the world. As the presence of God, once seen by Christianity as being separate from the world, is drawn into the world, it will suffuse it with Divine presence. As mentioned, the East has a tendency to separate from involvement with the world and the lives of others. The Hindu and Yogic tradition can both benefit from acknowledging that there is work to be done by us grassroots practitioners. There are added spiritual responsibilities to be embraced, in which we play a more active role in making our world, and the consciousness of our species, more representative of the enlightened states. Many Hindu gurus have undertaken this role; however, the most effective form of transformation is possible only when the everyday practitioner shares the responsibilities, and this should happen around the world, India included. Through the marriage of East and West, we may embrace the vision of original sin transformed into original blessing[9] and see the world as the ancients once saw it: at once physical, psychological, *and* spiritual. The purpose of recovering this vision is to help usher in the new world order that Jesus identified as the kingdom of God, which was also Israel's vision of a new creation truly fulfilled in God. Jesus's essential message, "The time is now! Repent, for the Kingdom of God is at hand" (Mark 1:15), can easily be translated into Yogic language as "Turn within, spiritual enlightenment is within your power, now." Bourgeault interpreted *metanoia*, the Greek word used in place of *repent* in early translations, to also signify "going beyond the mind,"[10] an esoteric translation that is not only close to the literal meaning of the word but also identical to the literal meaning and purpose of the word *mantra*.

If the ultimate meaning and purpose of life is to be found in the kingdom-of-God experience, which is best understood as an ultimate state of consciousness, then this beatific vision, the one that Arjuna beholds in the Bhagavad Gita, and that many of the great Christian saints have experienced, is the real heart of both traditions. In this final state, Bede Griffiths explains, "the human body will be totally penetrated by spiritual consciousness and become a 'spiritual body,' and at the same time the material world with all its energies now penetrated by [supreme] consciousness will become a 'new creation.'"[11] The great Indian mystic Shri Aurobindo, another visionary who sought to synthesize East and West, shares a similar vision of a transformed existence, which he describes in his work *The Life Divine*.[12] Interestingly, Shri Aurobindo used the term *Integral Yoga* to define the process by which this vision could be brought about, a term that can be elaborated on in the continued dialogue between Yoga and Christianity.

It is important to acknowledge that Eckhart Tolle, Wayne Dyer, Caroline Myss, and all the other wonderful teachers of the present spiritual order in the West are helping usher in this consciousness, as are the great contemporary spiritual teachers of the East, including luminaries such as Shri Shri Ravi Shankar, Sadhguru Jaggi Vasudev, and Amma. In individuals such as these, it is easy to see the

Christ Self shining through them, defying all attempts at definition. All of us are called to help usher in this consciousness, and we must each be actively engaged in the process. One way to start is through conversations with other traditions: Yogis can open their Yoga studios to dialogue sessions, so that individuals from Christian groups can come to exchange views and teachings, and church groups can be open to sessions of respectful dialogue in the spirit of learning and mutual exchange. In actually sharing physical space with a person, we can sense the innate goodness and sincerity in the other, and everyone is enriched in the process.

Let me reiterate that my vision is not for Yogis or Hindus to become, through this process, Christians, or for Christians to become Hindus. It is not my intention to convert anyone to either path. Nor am I suggesting a homogenous mixture that conveniently puts Yoga and Christianity together. My hope, as stated earlier, is that Christians and Hindus heal some of the wounds that have been generated by intolerance, lack of knowledge, and prejudice. These wounds run deep, even today; our world will be better off when they are healed, and our human family will be stronger for it.

I, for my part, would like to be authentically Hindu and authentically Christian at the same time and I can only hope that, because I seek to live both traditions sincerely (albeit imperfectly), both traditions will want to claim me as their own, as happened to the Indian mystic Kabir, mentioned at the start of this chapter. It has been done by Father Bede Griffiths (also known as Swami Dayananda), by Father Henri Le Saux, OSB (also known as Swami Abishkitananda), by Brother Wayne Teasdale (also known as Paramatmananda), and by countless unrecorded others.[13] In fact, such integration is now surfacing in a model that may be our hope for the future: interspirituality. This term, coined by my good friend the late Wayne Teasdale, refers to our ability to sincerely live more than one tradition simultaneously. The Divine is more than one tradition, and we, at our core, are destined to become "world souls" in which the essence of the world's great traditions can coalesce and burn as brightly as any supernova.

Epilogue

WE ARE JUST BEGINNING to sense the value of interspirituality, which can be seen, first, as a state of living more than one spiritual tradition authentically, and second, as the incorporation into one's own tradition of what is better developed in another tradition. There is sufficient momentum for interspirituality in the groundwork established by many of the pioneering figures I mentioned earlier, such as Griffiths and Teasdale, as well as such individuals as Rev. Matthew Fox.

I sincerely hope that the resources, thoughts, ideas, and practices I presented in the previous chapters inspire you to take up the work and find some meaningful way to incorporate the vision of interspirituality into your life and community. I plan to publish other works to further illustrate the power of the interspiritual approach, drawing from various traditions, especially Christianity and Yoga.

I have deliberately chosen not to address, except in passing, the limitations, or "shadow side," of the East, because discussing it would have detracted from the main thrust of my message. But shadow does indeed exist in the East, in, for example, the distancing of oneself from the circumstances of others, which I mentioned in chapter 6, or the caste system or the autonomous authority of some gurus. However, abuse by some does not detract from the authenticity of others. We can say the same of Christianity and the Western world as well: there is much in both that is appreciable. In this epilogue I address a few points in support of this appreciation, especially since I have spoken of Christianity much like the boy who pointed out that the emperor had no clothes on. All of my observations and suggestions have been intended respectfully and must be kept in perspective, that is, not generalized.

Although many Hindus (and here I mean people from India) perceive a lack of spirituality in the West, a very large number of them desire to live and work here. While initially the allure is professional and financial opportunity, many Indians discover once they arrive that there is also a palpable spiritual power in the United States, which is seldom portrayed by American television, business, or politics. This spiritual power inheres in the people, the land, and the spiritual values that shape the people. Additionally, this power stems from the same source that once inspired the founders in the formation of this country. It has gradually shaped the American soul over the centuries, and is apparent today in the movement toward interspirituality, for which the United States is the world's laboratory. It's worth describing how I came to this understanding.

In the fifth year of monastic training at the ashram, I began to feel uncomfortable. A few years before this discomfort, I had undertaken a "simple profession," a three-year commitment during which one tries to discern whether or not one is being called to the life of a monk permanently. These "temporary" vows, as they are called, are renewed, sometimes twice, before one makes a "final profession" to devote the rest of one's life to upholding one's monastic vows to be alone with God and passionately seek Divine union. In addition to the classic vows of poverty, chastity, and obedience, Benedictine monks also take vows of stability and conversion. Poverty is the choice to live without any personal possessions; chastity the choice to live without a sexual partner or sexual indulgence. Obedience is the choice to give up one's will to the will of God, often mediated through the abbot and the community. Stability is the commitment to the specific geographic location of the monastery and its lifestyle, and conversion the commitment to constant inner change.

As I mentioned in chapter 3, the life of the monk revolves around the monastic *horarium*, the schedule. When I first arrived at the ashram and told Bede that I wished to become a monk, he responded, "Are you willing to give up having music as the center of your life and make contemplative prayer and the experience of God that center?" During the time of my temporary vows, I discovered that my strong artistic tendencies, such as sudden and sporadic spontaneity and long hours of extrapolating an idea, could not be regulated by a schedule. Creativity, like the wind, has a will of its own and is hard to predict. Over time, my creative impulses became overpowering. While it was necessary for me to control my creative urges in training as a monk, I later realized that creativity is a divine quality I can use to bring myself and others closer to the experience of God. Moreover, I fell in love. A beautiful Indian woman came to stay

at the monastery as a guest. She was, like me, a passionate
spiritual seeker, profoundly attracted to the ashram way
of life, and was from a strikingly similar background: a
Catholic family with Hindu ancestry and a deep fascina-
tion with Indian spirituality. Another reason for my discomfort was the idea of being a monk in the formal sense
of the word. People had expectations about how a monk
should walk, talk, and generally behave, and I found myself
playing to that role. A new image began to crystallize in
which I saw my calling to live outwardly as an ordinary person living a normal life in the world while inwardly cultivating the life of a mystic.

I spoke with Bede Griffiths, my mentor, and asked to
be freed from my vows in order to marry and move west.
Although I had received many invitations to come to the
United States, my mentor was not keen on the prospect.
Initially, he felt that living in the United States might
adversely affect my spiritual life. However, later, after allowing the move, he realized that it was indeed my calling
to be situated in the West. What he did discern rather
quickly was the spiritual potential of my marriage, and so he
performed the ceremony after a weeklong private retreat
with my wife-to-be and me in the mountains, even though
our parents were against it. After that, we spent close to six
months in the ashram as a married couple, during which
Bede spent several hours each day counseling us on how to
live out our marriage spiritually. His influence on us continues even now, almost twenty years since that time. I
should mention here that his recognition of the spiritual
potential of a married life was a definite shift in his thinking. Bede had lived as a celibate monk almost all his adult
life. Yet, with our marriage, he seemed, perhaps for the first

time, to regard married life in its totality as something that was comparable to the spiritual stature of the monk.

Additionally, after more than thirty-five years of living immersed in the spiritual culture of India, a context that Bede always felt was more spiritually inclined than the West, he now turned toward the Western world, especially after our departure from India. Even in the years before this, he had been sensing that something powerful was brewing in the West, spiritually, that is, and he had a strong feeling that this "spiritual renaissance" was concentrated in America. Once we arrived, he considered starting a spiritual community with us in the United States and spending part of the year here. In response to this vision, he would, each year, leave India and spend approximately a third of the year with my wife and me, traveling to various parts of the country and meeting with people and organizations. With each visit, it became more and more clear to him that future models of spirituality, especially interspirituality, are being birthed here in the spiritual laboratory of America. We postulated that *United States* could be a symbolic term for the "united states of consciousness." Sadly, he died after three annual visits, but only after planting many seeds here in the United States, in us and in the many he touched during his visits.

The Spiritual Power of the American Soul

There is something powerful about the American soul that expresses itself in openness, honesty, vulnerability, determination, and a childlike passion for learning that truly embodies the human spirit. This is what makes Americans the ideal students for any new spiritual system, and why so many Eastern teachers have found such fulfillment and appreciation in this country. Additionally, there is a sense of truth, justice, fairness, and accountability, and many an Eastern spiritual teacher and spiritual system has been subject to these principles of growth. It is this spiritual power, the combination of acceptance and challenge, that draws other cultures from around the world to come and live here, to be a part of this transformative energy field. It is now critical for the United States to not only develop its spiritual power as a model for the world but also rebuild trust and credibility with other nations. Knowledge, not just of other cultures but of other spiritualities too, is indispensable to building this trust. As Americans look hard at their economic and political situation and seek to become actively involved in their own transformation and the transformation of the world, it is vital that this interspiritual dimension be given value and attention. The classic European Christian profile of the past is too strongly associated with an image of the oppressor in the wake of colonialism and its accompanying aggressive missionary activities. Furthermore, the intention behind interspirituality is not conversion, but marriage in the symbolic sense.

As I have stated already, marriage not only requires each partner to be respectful of the other, to allow the other to be himself or herself, but to also challenge the other to grow in love. At the same time, one responds to challenges, taking the initiative to grow and change with the other. Most important, in marriage one does not quit the relationship on a whim, but stays the course because each partner is aware of the other's shadow even while remaining committed to the other's life, liberty, and right to happiness. This is the kind of relationship that the spiritual traditions of the world must commit to, and the success of such relationships lies not only in the hands of religious leaders but also in the hands of individuals. When large numbers of followers in a spiritual tradition push toward an ideal, the leaders will take notice, as has happened in the case of Christianity.

It is impressive that the most widely influential spiritual teachers in the Western world either are from the United States or Canada or are based there. In fact, the whole world is represented in the American melting pot, which is also a smithy where we are cooking and forging simultaneously. What is important is that these gurus of the West are taking the best of the East and integrating it with the best of the West, presenting the whole in a democratic format with a logical pedagogy grounded in science and balanced with psychology. The way American Yoga is developing is a classic example of this process. This is the new Western mission: integration, not conversion. In fact, many Indians today, Hindus in particular, are reading the books of Western teachers and following their teaching. I speak here of teachers such as Eckhart Tolle, Wayne Dyer, Carolyn Myss, Louise Hay, Shakti Gawain, and Deepak Chopra. Traditional Christianity is yet to develop a viable interspiritual form, but it is also doing its best to respond to the needs of our time. This is why the model of Shantivanam and the work of Bede Griffiths could prove to be invaluable.

The New Mission of Christianity

In response to the tension and violence between Hindus and Christians in India, one of the monks of Bede's monastery, John Martin Sahajananda, wrote the following statement as part of a twenty-point manifesto outlining a new mission for Christianity.

For us to become instruments of peace, that is, to embody the message of Jesus, we need to be free from any ambition of expanding our boundaries and increasing our numbers as Christians. For this to happen, we have to see everyone already in the kingdom of God and help them to discover this truth. This means renouncing religious conversions, for where there is a mission to convert there is a sort of violence, a violation of someone else's identity and core belief. This interior perspective of violence prevents us from becoming true instruments of peace.

To be instruments of peace in our world, we need to become spiritual liberators, and this requires that we stop being spiritual colonizers. Jesus was not a spiritual colonizer who wished to convert people to his authority and rule them. He was a spiritual liberator who came to make people free with his truth. Jesus emphatically proclaimed that "The Truth will make you free" (Jn. 8.14–15), and "I do not call you servants anymore, because a servant does not know what his master is doing. But I have called you friends, because I have made known to you everything that I have heard from my Father" (Jn. 15.15).

The way to becoming a spiritual liberator requires that we make the transition from being believers to becoming seekers, for remaining on the level of belief is the main source of conflict and violence. Jesus said, "Seek you first the kingdom of God and its righteousness and all things will be given unto you" (Mt. 6.33). Believing is only the starting point. Furthermore, we also need to have an inclusive vision of being Christian: a Christian is not someone who believes in Christ alone but someone who extends that belief to everyone who is searching for Truth or God or the kingdom of God.[1]

Reclaiming Spiritual Vulnerability

One point I must make in closing is that it is often hard for Hindus — and as a result some Western Yogis — to understand or appreciate spiritual vulnerability. Traditional Indian spirituality is about rising "above" our humanness and becoming purely divine, for that is our source and therefore our destiny. Jesus, for instance, should not have suffered if he was truly an avatar, the Divine descended to earth. Nevertheless, that is precisely the point. Jesus was a unique incarnation who came to reveal the fact that the Divine wants our love but has given us free will to choose to give or receive it. His physical and mental suffering reflected a divine process that would otherwise have evaded our notice, and it is this that sets him apart from the typical Hindu avatar, who is entirely God-like and therefore entirely nonhuman, which means without any discernable human frailties or limitations. Jesus is a combination of the complete human and the complete divine, which is something to be appreciated. Consider that Jesus says, "My God, my God, why have you deserted me?"(Matthew 27:46). How could he, if he were fully a god, ever say this? Even more poignant is his prayer "Father, all things are possible unto thee; remove this cup from me" (Mark 14:36).

The movie *Bruce Almighty* offers a profound glimpse into the human-Divine dynamic. In the story, Bruce does not think God is doing such a great job. So God, played by

Morgan Freeman, confers upon Bruce, played by Jim Car-
rey, all his divine powers for a limited time. However, one
rule he must follow is that he cannot mess with free will. In
the end, Bruce is disillusioned to find that, despite all his
power to impress everyone, he is unable to impress himself
and, more important, the love of his life, Grace (played by
Jennifer Anniston), who no longer wants to be in a relationship with him. When Bruce exasperatedly asks, "How
do I get her to love me?" God quietly replies, "You let me
know when you figure that one out." This may appear to be
a crude portrayal of the construction and purpose of the
universe, but it is a profound analogy. The Creator, at least
from the Christian and Jewish viewpoint, has deliberately
endowed us with the will to refuse to love him back or even
to appreciate any part of his creation, yet all the while he
sustains the environment in which we subsist, even the very
powers of our perception.

In the East, there is a tendency to assume that God
does not need our love, for God is complete. However, the
unique Christian and Jewish tradition states precisely that
the Divine really desires our love with *all* of its being. The
reason for Jesus's particular incarnation was to make it clear
that God has a love interest in us humans, and that God is
committed to seeing it through till the end, to its fulfillment. However, this fulfillment is not forced, for it involves
our choice in the matter. It would not be love otherwise.
True love requires us to interact with others with the possibility and potential of being rejected, and the classic Yogic
way is to be above pleasure and pain, which is to be inca-
pable of being hurt. Nevertheless, love hurts! So how do we
reconcile this truth with being a Yogi?

Many Hindus found it extremely difficult to accept, for

instance, that Mother Teresa seemed to have gone through a forty-year dark night of the soul, during which she felt deprived of Divine solace. In a press release dated September 17, 2007, published in several Indian newspapers, the well-known Indian guru Shri Shri Ravi Shankar declares, "Mother Teresa has done unparalleled service to India. Could she also have benefited from the unparalleled spiritual wealth of India? Yes, definitely!" If the church had officially sanctioned the practice of Eastern meditation, she certainly would have practiced it. Yet the witness of Mother Teresa is remarkable: that she could keep giving herself to others in love, despite the fact that she was not receiving spiritual consolations in her inner life. This Christian sense of other-centeredness warrants appreciation; while it can be limiting, it can also be commendable. However, there is a way for us to bring the best of both worlds together — mysticism and sanctity, inner-centeredness and outer-centeredness — and in the process, the East will truly appreciate what is at the heart of Jewish and Christian mysticism: relationship. This other-centeredness that exists at the grassroots level among everyday practitioners is the driving force in Western culture that can help balance the West's recovery of mysticism.

It never ceases to amaze me that, when someone is missing in the United States, hundreds of people will drop whatever they are doing and lend a hand to search for this person. Or that, after World War II, through the Marshall Plan, the United States helped to rebuild Germany, using citizens' hard-earned tax dollars and know-how to help the very people who had killed and wounded their fellow countrymen, threatened their security, and brought them economic hardship.[2] Without such other-centeredness, mysticism can all too easily become self-absorbed, especially in the early stages of spiritual formation. This has been the Catholic Church's fear about encouraging mysticism, as it can lead to narcissism on the one hand, or madness on the other. However, the suppression of the mystical dimension can, as we have seen, lead to its own problems, which is why we need a marriage of East and West. Bede Griffiths learned how to combine the two after growing up in the West and then living the rest of his life in the East. I am achieving this integration from the opposite direction, having grown up in the East and now living my spiritual life in the West. In this process, I have learned, much as my mentor did, that all my knowledge of Eastern spirituality and Yoga and meditation is worthless without love. Saint Paul, in his first letter to the Corinthians (13:1–13), sums it up beautifully:

If I speak in human and angelic tongues but do not have love, I am a resounding gong or a clashing cymbal.

And if I have the gift of prophecy and comprehend all mysteries and all knowledge; if I have all faith so as to move mountains but do not have love, I am nothing.

If I give away everything I own, and if I hand my body over so that I may boast but do not have love, I gain nothing.

Love is patient, love is kind. It is not jealous, [it] is not pompous, it is not inflated, it is not rude, it does not seek its own interests, it is not quick-tempered, it does not brood over injury, it does not rejoice over wrongdoing but rejoices with the truth.

Love bears all things, believes all things, hopes all things, endures all things.

Love never fails. If there are prophecies, they will be brought to nothing; if tongues, they will cease; if knowledge, it will be brought to nothing.

For we know partially and we prophesy partially, but when the perfect comes, the partial will pass away.

When I was a child, I used to talk as a child, think as a child, reason as a child; when I became [an adult], I put aside childish things.

At present we see indistinctly, as in a mirror, but then face to face. At present, I know partially; then I shall know fully, as I am fully known.

So faith, hope, love remain, these three; but the greatest of these is love.

Paraphrasing this well-known passage from a yogic perspective may read something like this:

If I were to chant proficiently in ancient Sanskrit or other sacred languages, but do not have love, I am a resounding gong or a clashing cymbal.

And if I can stand on my head, contort my body in extraordinary shapes, and be without breathing for hours, or claim to be Self-realized, but do not have love, I am nothing.

If I give away everything I own, renounce the world, dress in saffron, or cover my body in ash but do not have love, I gain nothing.

Love is patient, love is kind. It is not jealous, [it] is not pompous, it is not inflated, it is not rude, it does not seek its own interests, it is not quick-tempered, it does not brood over injury, it does not rejoice over wrongdoing but rejoices with the truth.

Love bears all things, believes all things, hopes all things, endures all things.

Love never fails. If there are great philosophies, they will be brought to nothing; metaphysical knowledge will be brought to nothing; even powerful meditation practices will cease.

For we know only partially and we perceive partially, but when the perfect comes, the partial will pass away.

At present we see indistinctly, as in a mirror, but then face to face. At present, I know partially; then I shall know fully, as I am fully known.

So while chanting and yoga practice and philosophy and meditation may all remain, the greatest of these is love.

Salvation and Enlightenment

I have suggested in this book that Christians should not require that the profession of salvation through Jesus be the starting point for Hindus and Yogis and other Eastern practitioners interested in learning the Christian way. There is a large group of people, both in India and in the West, for whom this statement is a complete turn-off. An approach should also be available to estranged Christians, because belief in salvation is one that a person must come to as a realization from within, through a process of maturation.

Christian salvation is different from, but comparable to, the enlightenment of the East. Original sin, rather than being an act, is better understood as a "potentiality." This potentiality, although expressible through any number of

acts with any number of variations, is the key to understanding how we can effectively wrestle with the most powerful barrier between our Creator and us. Moreover, Yoga,
if understood properly in this context, can be the bridge to
this understanding. As humans, as individuals, as communities, and as a species, we must come to the conscious realization that we have the power to deny the Spirit of God
within us, which is to refuse to accept or give love. Without
this potentiality, we would be automatons, programmed to
accomplish the will of God and to love each other without
any choice in the matter. This is why, as I explain in chapter 4, the fall from Eden was necessary and is actually a
blessing, especially when this potentiality is used to respond
to love rather than to reject it. It is only through love that
the world and our existence take on meaning and purpose.

We, as a species, were designed for "love by choice,"
which is modeled on the power of our Creator, God himself. The message that Christians have inferred from Jesus's
death is that, despite how we use this potentiality, either to
accept or reject love, God still loves us and is always waiting for our response like a loving parent. This loving and
waiting are both individual and collective, and this is the
true promise of salvation. God does not, and will not at
some point, get fed up and walk away from the relationship. The parable of the prodigal son makes this clear. God
is not waiting to punish our turning away from love, but is
always waiting patiently to love us into turning toward
goodness, which is the prerequisite for love. Furthermore,
we cannot bargain with love, not even spiritually. The parable of the workers in the fields is telling in this regard.
Someone who has put in very little effort, turning toward
God at the end of his or her life, may end up with exactly

the same fruit of Divine union as those who have loved God all their lives, because the love of the Spirit is always constant and full for everyone, without discrimination. It is we who do all the calculating and scheming and strategizing.

The message that we infer from Jesus's life and death is the revelation, the purpose, and the configuration of this great love. This is the theology of the Holy Trinity, which, like any theological model, is awkward, for we are using human language to comprehend transpersonal mystery. The underlying message, though, is quite simple. The Trinity is trying to communicate that there is a dynamic relationship at the heart of ultimate reality. In other words, ultimate reality, which Hindus refer to as Brahman,[3] is present in everything, in every process, and contains within itself a dynamic relationship in love. This is the heart of the Christian and Jewish revelations, this knowledge and the invitation to each one of us to join in this relationship — or banquet, as Jesus often referred to it, for the relationship "feeds" us. He used many allusions, such as "living water" and "bread of life," to signify that we are nourished by this relationship. It does not matter whether Jesus consciously knew that he was meant to deliver this message from God to the world, but it is crucial that humanity realize it. The message is this: God loves the world so much that he or she or it is always willing to be humiliated and take a backseat to our egos while continuing to patiently await our return to love, like the father of the prodigal son. This is also the message of Jesus's coming to call out to the lost sheep, for no one (however deliberately they might deny the presence of Spirit) is placed outside the circle of God's love, which encompasses and embraces all things as much as it is located within all things.

This is why, when a Christian conservative says that he or she is "saved," I now understand the premise this person is operating from, and I respect it. I also understand why he or she wants to communicate this message to the rest of the world. It is indeed a liberating message to know that true fulfillment is not only possible through many lifetimes of spiritual effort and discipline but also through a simple opening in love that makes transparent the dynamic relationship of our being in love with God, and God's being in love with us. Jesus's message is that, despite one's accumulation of bad karma for many lifetimes, a single act of utter transparency that completely opens the mind and heart and depths of one's soul to God is all it takes for the fullness of realization that can be sustained by grace. This is why I can only hope that neither Yoga practitioners nor Hindus reject the message altogether, for there is a profound truth to it, despite its awkward language.

Accepting the central thesis of Christianity need not involve giving up one's culture or spiritual tradition, and Christianity must find a way to invite others into the deepest aspects of its tradition without requiring them to give up what is holy and essential to their well-being. It would not help if the whole world were to become Christian, or Hindu, at the expense of the rest of the world's spiritual traditions. We need the balance that comes from the dynamic relationship of each with one another, Islam included, and should perhaps see them as all integrated into a sort of spiritual ecosystem, with all of them necessary for the health of the whole.

I hope this work helps in some manner to heal the relationship between Yogis (and Hindus) and Christians while, at the same time, inspiring each to respond to the challenges that the others present through their individual emphases.

I wish you well on your journey...

In One Spirit,

Russill Paul
Austin, Texas
December 17, 2008

Interspiritual Practices, Resources, and Select Bibliography

IN THIS SECTION, I share some of my personal practices that I offer in my workshops and retreats across the country. I offer them here only as a model. You can, of course, create your own meaningful practices, depending on your needs, your taste, and your community. I also invite you to make the journey to the Shantivanam ashram, Bede Griffiths's monastery in India, which is still functioning. If you wish, you can join me and a group of pilgrims from the United States and Canada who make the journey there each year. These are a mixture of Yogis, Christians, Jews, and Buddhists who, over a three-week period, pray together, chant together, visit temples together, and explore the depth of interspiritual dialogue through life at Shantivanam, where it all began for me.

Although many spiritual seekers today choose to avoid formal participation in religion, there are valuable aspects to conventional religions, and these are important to preserve and embrace. Moreover, it is important that those who seek to further their development by charting new territory not look down on those who find comfort and meaning in traditional forms.

Seeking union with the Divine as a practicing Christian or Hindu means that you align yourself with literally millions of other believers, that you have access to thousands of years of spiritual wisdom, and that you do not travel the spiritual path entirely alone. Therefore, when a Christian walks into a yoga studio for the first time, he or she needs to sense that behind the leotards stands a five-thousand-year history of development. Similarly, when a Yoga practitioner enters a church or synagogue, he or she must understand that behind what may be perceived as rote action stands a history of development that must be honored. We all need to guard against judging too quickly. The first step on either side is acceptance and the honoring of the rich tradition and history behind the existing forms. There is, however, an interesting tension, as evident in the theme of this book. Those who seek to blend traditions must do this sensitively, without simply mixing and matching. However, those who adhere to conventional forms must be tolerant of the fact that some mixing and matching may be necessary to achieve more sensitive blends.

On the one hand, many today feel a desperate need to connect with the Divine essence that exists independently of religions and spiritual traditions. On the other hand, we cannot do away with established religion. Religious traditions, as forms, really do matter, and one can't dismiss them altogether or take them apart and recombine them in an effort to get in touch with the Divine essence, and then discard them. This may sound like a contradiction, one that challenges anyone who wants to blend the two traditions:

one must reconcile the apparent conflict as well as learn to live with the tensions. The tension, however, is the way to, and offers the inspiration for, growth and maturity. Many aspects of the reconciliation are implicit in the points I make throughout this book. Here, I seek to illustrate them through examples. These examples may or may not work for others exactly as I practice them, such as my use of Sanskrit for my prayer life. However, the principle or intention behind the practice can still be adopted. For instance, to recover a sense of mystery in prayer experience, one can choose Gaelic or Latin in place of Sanskrit. But for those who want to explore a distinctively Yogic Christian experience, this chapter offers some useful possibilities.

To understand the value of what we undertake in the blending of Yoga and Christianity, consider language. Sure, it would be nice to communicate telepathically and dispense with language altogether, but as social beings without that capability, we need language to communicate. Languages are, in one sense, all the same: they are cultural technologies that enable communication. However, in another sense, languages are completely different, because each one envelops its speaker in a unique system of meaning-making that shapes cognition and perception. Religions are very similar in that regard. Each one offers a different conduit to God; you need at least one such conduit to make the connection. But there's nothing about the nature of religions-as-conduits that says you can't use more than one. As you can see, this extended comparison helps build the analogy that embracing more than one religion is like speaking more than one language. Among other things, this analogy offers a way of explaining the attitudinal shift needed to reduce conflict among religions in the world.

Chapter 1 Exercises:
Christianity's Domestication of God

Take a few moments to ask yourself how you experience God. Is God an all-too-familiar person or idea, or is there a sense of mystery about God? What do you do to experience God as mystery?

Have you closely observed the relationship between the food you eat and your inner life? Try starting a journal in which you record the sorts of thoughts and emotions you have during the week, and make a note of your diet. Another week, deliberately avoid these foods and foods with high sugar content, carbonated drinks, and drinks with too much caffeine. Limit your alcohol intake, or just stay away from it altogether. Decrease your meat, fish, and poultry intake by eating these foods less often or in smaller portions. Try to eat only free-range meats and poultry and organic products. Drink lots of purified water. Compare your thoughts, your emotions, and your inner connection to the Divine that result from this diet with those of the previous week.

Have you ever been to a yoga class? Go to a local yoga studio and just hang out for a bit. Talk to someone, either a student or a teacher. Try to get a sense of this person. Do you feel God's presence flowing in him or her? Is this person sincere about what he or she is doing? Consider taking a beginning yoga class.

If you are a Yoga practitioner, do a short meditation on the New Testament. Start with the Gospel of John, which is a profoundly mystical read. Read slowly and without judgment. If a phrase strikes you, stop and think about it. Ask how you can integrate its message into your Yoga practice. Find a way to understand it in Yogic language. If you are a Yoga teacher, consider drawing a parallel and including it in your Yoga class.

Chapter 2 Exercises: Seeking the Essence

Take an hour or two off on the weekend and try and enter into an experience of essence. Relax your mind and stay present with whatever you are doing. If it makes you more comfortable, preface your practice with "I now sink into the exploration of God's being. May the Holy Spirit guide me." After that, use a simple phrase or word to stay focused, such as *washing hands* or *eating*. Do whatever you do much slower than you normally would, so that you can take in all the nuances of the experience.

If you do not have an hour or two of free time, take a five- to ten-minute break during your workweek to seek out the experience of essence. The washroom is actually a convenient place in which to do spiritual practice, because of the privacy it offers us. When there, take your time as you wash your hands and simply experience all the sensation that accompanies the experience. You can also do this while showering (that is, before starting your workday), by using the word *showering* to bring your awareness to all the sensations you are experiencing, instead of being preoccupied with the thoughts and images going on in your mind. You will find that this awareness effortlessly leads to an intense experience of your own presence that captures the quality of essence, which is the experience of your essential nature. It is through this awareness of our essential nature that we tap into the nature of God as Spirit, which in turn unfolds into our spiritual awakening and enlightenment.

Have you experienced your own essence? Do you only know yourself through your personality and its traits? Do you sense that there is something more to who you are? What is the nature of your soul? Do you feel that you are in touch with it? How often do you seek to know yourself in your essence?

Chapter 3 Exercises:
Melding Traditions from the East and West

One way to explore the benefits from the use of the mantra — that is, if you haven't done so before — is to take a word or phrase in any language. Start by saying it aloud so that you hear it spoken in the room. Feel its intrinsic rhythm as you say it repeatedly. After a while, whisper the same word or phrase and experience how your breath infuses the sound. Next, go inside your body and locate the sense of space around your heart. Now begin to say the same word or phrase internally. This time, however, pay more attention to the gap between your utterances and the silence and stillness that fill that space.

Let us assume that you chose the word *love*. In the beginning, you are going to chant "love, love, love" over and over again, like a mantra. Or you might choose to say, "God is love." (However, try not to think about "how" God is love or why you feel that God is love. That's a different exercise.) Then, when you start whispering the word, draw in a slow, deep breath and whisper the word sensually, allowing your breath to infuse each utterance. Just experience the sound of the words. When you go inside your heart space and start to take in the silence and stillness that fill your being, you may experience the gentle heaving of your breath as your body breathes. Notice if you can sense a "presence" as well. Try to increase the length of the pauses between your utterances, and hold them as long as thoughts and images do not encroach on the stillness and silence. Try to sense the presence more strongly.

You can also do this with the name of Jesus, or with a word like *Abba*, the Aramaic word Jesus used to relate to God as Father. Or you can choose *Shree Ma*, the Sanskrit for Holy Mother. The point is to allow the word to lead you into an experience of what the word stands for. The word is like a signpost that points to a certain reality. We have gotten so used to communicating *about* the signposts themselves that we often miss the realities they point to.

How do you use words? Are they just labels or terms? Do they connect you to experiences? Do you stay in your head when you discuss spiritual matters, or can you feel as well? Can you sustain a sense of experience without your mind and its images taking over in a manner that dilutes or distracts from the experience? What do you do to discipline your mind? How successful are you in this discipline?

Chapter 4 Exercises:
Finding Unity with the Divine

Here are a couple of powerful Sanskrit Christian mantras that have greatly enhanced my Yoga practice. Try using them with the technique described above.

The first is "Om namah Christaaya," the *namajapa* we chanted in the predawn hours at Shantivanam, which I describe in chapter 3. *Namaha* is from the same root as *namaste* — *nam* — which literally means "to bow, to bend, to prostrate" and, therefore, signifies worship and adoration. *Christaaya* is the word for Christ, meaning "to the anointed one." In English, then, the mantra can be taken to mean "I bow to Christ, the anointed One" or "I worship the living presence of the anointed One." Ask yourself, "What would it feel like to be anointed by God?"

Another mantric prayer is "Yesu, Yesu, jai jai namo." It is in the same meter as "Shri Rama jaya Rama jaya jaya Rama," except here we have the name of Jesus. *Yesu* is the Sanskrit for Jesus and is very close to the Aramaic *Yeshua*, only lighter and therefore more soothing. *Namo* is from the same root as *nam*. Since Jesus was a great healer, I use this mantra whenever I am in need of healing, either emotional or spiritual. Ask yourself, "What would it be like to experience Jesus as a healer? If he were offering a session, would I go? Would I experience this healing if I lovingly called upon his name?"

Try using the syllable *Ye* (rhyming with *day*) as you sense your body inhale, and *Su* (as in *Sue*) as you sense your body exhale. Allow your breathing to be natural, and say the sounds internally with your eyes closed. There is a natural rhythm to the sound of the breath that resonates closely with the sound of this mantra. Use it to calm yourself, comfort yourself, or soothe yourself to sleep. Of course, you can also use it to enter into the awareness of the "presence" of Jesus. Another powerful breath prayer is the phrase *So-Ham*, which in Sanskrit means "That [Divine Spirit] I am." If it makes you more comfortable, you can preface your practice by saying "God is" or "I am in God" and then use the mantra to enter into the presence of that experience.

The loftiest purpose of any mantra is to help you find unity with the Divine and, through that unity, discover the Divine nature. How often do you seek the Divine for its own sake? Have you experienced the Divine nature? What is it like for you? Are you curious enough to want to experience more of it, or have you decided that what you've experienced is enough?

Chapter 5 Exercises: Charting a Path

Each one of us charts his or her path somewhat differently. I like using the Sanskrit Christian prayers with yoga postures and simple prayerful movements drawn from the Sufi tradition. One simple way to do this is to spread your arms wide and turn slowly while you chant. Sufis call this the "remembrance of God." And they like to say that, when they turn, they are "returning" to God by "turning toward" God. The result, they claim, is that they discover themselves turning "with God" and "in God." You could use Sanskrit chants, or you can choose Latin or Greek or Aramaic. The simpler the phrase, the easier to quiet the mind and enter into the experience of contemplation through movement.

If you are a Yoga practitioner, you may want to try a Latin chant such as "Spiritus Sanctus," which means "Holy Spirit." There is an interesting resonance between the words *Parashakti* (the Yogic equivalent of "Holy Spirit") and *Paraclete*, the word used by Christians when referring to the Holy Spirit. (*Paraclete* comes from a Greek word meaning "one who consoles, one who intercedes on our behalf, a comforter or an advocate.")[1] There is a strong resonance here with the word *Agni* as well, referring to the power of fire, which, as described in the Vedas, intercedes between humans and the Divine. At Pentecost, when the Holy Spirit came upon the disciples of Jesus, it came with the sound "of a rushing mighty wind" and took the form of "cloven tongues like as of fire" sitting upon each of them individually. Pentecost was a Jewish harvest feast for which the disciples were gathered. This can be seen as a communal Yogic experience, even a manifestation of kundalini, that we can, as Yoga practitioners, seek to experience today.

As a Yoga practitioner, have you ever wondered what Jesus's mystical experience was like? Are you curious enough to seek it for yourself? How would you compare his experience with the deepest experiences recorded in Yogic texts? What are some of the most valuable teachings of the gospel that you would be willing to undertake as part of your Yoga *sadhana* (discipline)? What do you think it would involve to taste the mystical experience of Jesus through your Yoga practice?

Chapter 6 Exercises:
Yoga and the Revitalization of Christianity

We each have to find innovative methods to revitalize our spiritual lives and, through this process, revitalize our communities. When I presented a retreat in Louisville, Kentucky, in spring 2008, I was interviewed by an amazing group of teens called PeaceCasters. This project is coordinated by the Center for Interfaith Relations in Louisville. The purpose of the program is to help teens understand other traditions and allow them to shoot videos, edit them, and then publish their video clips to spread peace in the world. Seeing these kids involved in interspiritual work at such a tender age is heartwarming. All kids are interested in technology, so a program through which they can creatively learn from different faith traditions is powerful. They get to find their own voices while expanding their spiritual perspectives and spreading their awareness to others in their peer circle. In their own words, the project is about "kids coming together to avoid judging others for their faith," "breaking down the walls," "spreading messages of peace throughout the world through digital media," and "a vision of a peaceful world in which everyone can learn to work together." Their work is available for viewing on YouTube.com (keyword: peacecasters). Perhaps you can start something similar in your own region for youth or adults or both to inspire an interest in interspiritual dialogue.

Influential Yoga Systems

The Kripalu and Sivananda approaches to Yoga are among the best and most comprehensive in world. Not only do students learn the authentic heritage of Yoga, but they are also exposed to other perspectives in depth. If you are a Christian seeking to expand your spirituality to include Yoga, look for a Sivananda- or Kripalu-trained yoga teacher.

The Sivananda Yoga Vedanta Centers (http://sivananda.org). Swami Sivananda, a saint and renowned sage and humanitarian, is the inspiration behind the Sivananda Yoga Vedanta Centers, which have been, from their inception, involved in interspiritual dialogue. All of his direct disciples continued in the same vein, particularly Swami Vishnu-Devananda, who founded the International Sivananda Yoga Vedanta Centers and was a tireless campaigner for world peace. This organization regularly offers interspiritual conferences and ensures that Yoga teachers who participate in their programs are exposed to a wealth of world spiritualities.

Kripalu Center for Yoga and Health (www.kripalu.org) is perhaps the most prominent yoga-training center in North America. Its mission is to offer the authentic yoga experience free from any limiting cultural components. At the same time, Kripalu yoga teachers and practitioners are evenly exposed to a wide range of spiritual perspectives. The idea is that each individual can shape his or her own path in direct relationship to the Spirit within. This allows someone from a formal Christian background to experience yoga in a completely nonthreatening way. Located at what was once a Jesuit seminary, this is an undeclared interspiritual laboratory of the utmost importance.

Yoga-Practicing Catholic Priests and Monks

Father Anthony Randazzo, who serves the community of Notre Dame Roman Catholic Church in North Caldwell, New Jersey, has put together a program of yoga postures with the beatitudes. He offers retreats and programs based on *Beatitudes, Christ, and the Practice of Yoga*, a book he wrote with Maddalena Ferrara-Mattheis, a yoga teacher at Starseed Yoga in Montclair, New Jersey.

Father Thomas Ryan, a Paulist retreat facilitator, teaches "Yoga prayer," which enables the individual to rediscover the embodiment of the Christian spirit through yoga. His DVD *Yoga Prayer* demonstrates his particular style of Christian-based yoga practice. You can learn more about it at www.tomryancsp.org.

Brother Rolph Fernandes, a native of Trinidad, was a Franciscan monk for forty-three years. His main ministry for the Franciscan Order was Inter-Faith Dialogue. He was a founding member of the Interfaith Council of Montreal. Since 2000, he has been sharing his experiences in Inter-Faith Dialogue and Franciscan spirituality, offering retreats and lectures around the world on Yoga and Christianity, and Yoga and the spirit of Saint Francis. You can learn more about him at www.two-sandals.org.

Interspiritual Organizations

The Center for Interfaith Relations (www.interfaithrelations .org) not only coordinates the PeaceCasters project for teens and other interspiritual activities but also organizes an annual Festival of Faiths (www.festivaloffaiths.org) in Louisville, Kentucky. Perhaps your church or yoga center could do something similar in your area once a year.

Interspiritual Dialogue 'n Action (www.isdna.org) is a dynamic network that was formed in 2005. It is composed of various constituencies and groups inspired by the work and writing of Brother Wayne Teasdale, whose life was dedicated to the inspiration of interspiritual dialogue. It aims to carry forward to a worldwide audience his vision of interspiritual dialogue and interspirituality as outlined in his influential book *The Mystic Heart: Finding a Universal Spirituality in the World's Religions*. Teasdale, a Christian monk who took a Sanskrit name, Paramatmananda, meaning "Bliss of the Supreme Spirit," sought to hold both his Christian faith and his Hindu sensitivities in balance till the end of his life, in 2004.

The Council for a Parliament of World Religions (www .parliamentofreligions.org) was revived at its centenary celebration in 1993 to cultivate harmony among the world's religious and spiritual communities and to encourage their engagement with the world and its guiding institutions in order to achieve a just, peaceful, and sustainable world. It is a wonderful organization to join. It conducts conferences regularly and does much to advance deeper appreciation among established spiritual traditions and to foster a mutual trust and collaborative activity between faiths.

The Bede Griffiths International Trust (www.bedegriffiths .org) oversees the promulgation of Father Bede's vision in various ways: through making available his books, articles, and recordings (and those of other spiritual teachers as well); through retreats and contemplative prayer groups; through operation of the Bede Griffiths website; and through publication of the *Golden String* bulletin. Additionally, it promotes the awareness and practice of contemplative prayer, helping people to dispose themselves to receive the grace of contemplation, which, Father Bede believed, is offered to everyone, and which nurtures a spirit of peace and compassion among the peoples of the earth. The Camaldolese Institute for East-West Dialogue works with the trust to continue the pioneering work of Father Bede in the area of interreligious dialogue.

Creation Spirituality (www.creationspirituality.info). I have been blessed to have worked closely with the Reverend Matthew Fox for about sixteen years. Through his Creation Spirituality movement, I learned to appreciate the earth and the human body more than I can ever express. Matthew's vision is not only powerfully interspiritual but also reaches out to the young and disenfranchised through the Techno Cosmic Mass, a multimedia interspiritual ritual based on the traditional Catholic Mass, and the Yellawe Project, which trains youth in interspirituality, especially with an eye to awakening the mystic in them.

Contemplative Prayer Organizations

The World Community for Christian Meditation (www .wccm.org) was founded by Father Laurence Freeman. Father Laurence was a disciple of Father John Main, who had studied Eastern meditation with a great Indian Yogi, Swami Satyananda Saraswati. This organization helps Christians understand the value of contemplative prayer and introduces them to an effective method. It also helps individuals form local groups in their area to meet on a regular basis and develop the contemplative dimension in their lives. The group offers a wide range of products through its publishing arm, Medio Media (which has published a number of Bede Griffiths's books) and regularly organizes conferences, many of which encourage interfaith and interspiritual dialogue. The John Main method of using the mantra, extrapolated by his successor, Father Laurence, is an excellent method for Christians who are interested in techniques for practicing Eastern meditation but are concerned that it may compromise their faith.

Contemplative Outreach (www.centeringprayer.com) is a highly respected organization in North America founded by Father Thomas Keating, perhaps the most influential figure today among those helping Christians in the United States and Canada rediscover their contemplative mystical life through the practice of centering prayer. This organization also offers an array of resources as well as conferences. Keating's numerous books are a treasure house for Christians seeking to understand and develop the contemplative life, as well as for non-Christians who may be interested in understanding the deeper, mystical aspects of Christianity. Father Keating integrates a profound understanding of human psychology and levels of consciousness, which is crucial for Christians who want to expand their inner experience of the mystery of Christ.

Helpful Websites

If you are a yoga practitioner looking for an organization that truly embodies the spirit of love, see www.karmakrew.org.

If you are a Christian trying to find support among other Christians practicing yoga, you might consider visiting and perhaps joining www.christianspracticingyoga.com.

Another excellent resource is www.innerexplorations.com, a website hosted by James Arraj, who, together with his wife, Tyra, has been quietly engaged in interspiritual work. The two have produced a number of audio, video, and literary resources that they offer on their website, in addition to a wide selection of articles and interviews.

The Integral Institute (www.integralinstitute.org) was created by Ken Wilber, who is perhaps the most influential cross-cultural thinker today. Integral theory is an all-inclusive framework that draws on the key insights of the world's greatest knowledge traditions. The awareness gained from drawing on all truths and perspectives allows the integral thinker to bring new depth, clarity, and compassion to every level of human endeavor — from unlocking individual potential to finding new approaches to global-scale problems.

Interspiritual Models

In looking for inspiration for interspiritual models, I have found three templates already in place that I can recommend:

the Bahá'í Faith, Creation Spirituality, and the Unity movement.

The Bahá'í Faith

The Bahá'í faith, which is among the world's youngest religions, was founded in the eighteenth century by Bahá'u'lláh, a mystic and prophet born in Iran whose life ended, after much travel and gathering of wisdom, at the foot of Mount Carmel. The Bahá'ís recognize God's messengers in all the world's traditions, including Abraham, Moses, the Buddha, Zoroaster, Jesus, and Muhammad.

The central theme of this extraordinary messenger is that all of humanity is one single race and that the day has come for its unification in one global society, a message I truly relate to. As Bahá'u'lláh predicted, historical forces set in motion by God are breaking down traditional barriers of race, class, creed, and nation, and birthing a universal civilization. However, the principal challenge facing the peoples of the earth is to accept the fact of their oneness. Yoga and the central message of Hinduism are very similar; however, the Bahá'í faith offers its own special knowledge and resources to help make this possible. Roughly five million Bahá'ís — comprising a diverse group of races, nationalities, and cultures — work tirelessly around the world to realize Bahá'u'lláh's vision in the world today. Their goal: to propagate and inspire the vision of humanity as one global family and the earth as one homeland.

The Bahá'ís outline a very practical philosophy that asks its adherents to relinquish all forms of prejudice; ensure that women have the same opportunities as men and are valued equally; recognize that there is both unity and relativity in the notion of religious truth; strive to eliminate the extremities of both poverty and wealth; recognize the value of everyone's right to education; realize that each person is personally responsible for his or her independent search for the truth; seek to establish a global commonwealth of nations; and recognize that true religion is not in conflict but in harmony with reason and the pursuit of scientific knowledge.[2]

You may learn more at www.bahai.org and www.austin bahai.org

Creation Spirituality

While living as a monk at Shantivanam, I was fortunate to read *Original Blessing* by Matthew Fox. Bede was powerfully affected by the book, which forms the centerpiece of the Creation Spirituality movement. I was deeply moved by the book as well, and little did I know that in 1990, while traveling with Bede in America, we would meet the author, and that I would be invited to be part of his work and ministry.

The Reverend Fox, as he is now known, is a well-known Episcopalian priest, theologian, and educator. A former Dominican priest, Matthew spent many years trying to get the Catholic Church, and Christianity as a whole, to awaken to mysticism, feminist theology, liberation theology, and the value of indigenous spiritualities in contemporary times. As a result he was silenced by the Vatican, an act that only increased the visibility of his work in the public eye. Matthew's work helped me greatly. I learned much from him and from a pool of renowned faculty members of his spirituality programs, with whom I served for more than a decade and a half.

In seeking to connect with creation-centered Christian mysticism, Yogis and non-Christian spiritual seekers, as well as Christians who are unfamiliar with this tradition, ought to explore the writings of Meister Eckhart, Mechtilde of Magdeburg, Nicholas of Cusa, Julian of Norwich, and most importantly, Hildegard von Bingen, who was a brilliant musician, artist, and healer. These great mystics offer a depth and vision that complements the ascetic approaches of St. Anthony of the Desert and such later ascetics as St. John of the Cross and St. Teresa of Avila, who used the same traditional Christian way of purgation, illumination, and union that I used during my life as a monk. While this traditional Christian framework has strong parallels with the classic Yogic approach, the Creation Spirituality approach offers a variation.

Principles of Creation Spirituality

1. The universe is essentially a blessing, that is, something we intrinsically experience as good.

2. We are all naturally connected to the universe, as we are a microcosm of that macrocosm, which is why we should seek to nurture and develop this relationship more and more.

3. Everyone is a mystic, for we are all born full of wonder and capable of recovering it at any age, and this entails that we never take the awe and wonder of our existence for granted.

4. Humans have the obligation to dig and work hard at finding their deep self, their true self, their spirit self; thus the role of spiritual praxis and meditation and community confrontation which can itself be a yoga. In this way, we live and understand salvation as a way of "preserving the good." If we do not undergo such praxis, we live superficially out of fear or greed or addiction or someone else's expectations of us.

5. Everyone is an artist in some way, and Art, when used as meditation, is a primary form of prayer for releasing our images and empowering the community and each of us. This type of artistry finds its ultimate fulfillment in ritual, the community's art.

6. Everyone is a prophet, that is, a "mystic in action" who is called to "interfere" with whatever interrupts the authenticity of life, whenever that loss of connection is discerned, and wherever it may occur.

7. The journey of spiritual transformation can be named as a four-fold journey that includes all of the above, the wonder of the mystic, the depth search for the true self, the meditative power of art, and the social intervention of the prophet:

   Via Positiva: delight, awe, wonder, revelry
   Via Negativa: darkness, silence, suffering, letting go
   Via Creativa: birthing, creativity
   Via Transformativa: compassion, justice, healing, celebration.

8. We all have divine birthright, for we are all sons and daughters of God. We therefore have divine blood in our veins, divine breath in our lungs, and the obligation to do the basic work of God: Compassion.

9. Our sense of Divinity is to be all-embracing: as much Mother as Father, as much Child as Parent, as much Godhead (mystery) as God (history), as much beyond all beings as in all beings.

10. We need to supplant theism, and its child, atheism, with Panentheism, which is to experience that the Divine is in all things and all things in the Divine, and through this mystical intuition learn to relate to the Divine and experience the Sacred.[3]

You may learn more by visiting www.creationspirituality .info.

The Unity Movement

The Unity movement was founded by Charles and Myrtle Fillmore. After Myrtle Fillmore was remarkably healed using prayer and affirmations, many became interested in how she accomplished this healing. From small prayer circles in living rooms, Unity grew.

Unity is a refreshing approach to Christian spirituality because it emphasizes positivity in mental attitude and couples this with a practical and progressive approach to Christianity. Although the teachings of Jesus are central, it is the mystical dimension to his teaching that is most valued. In addition, Unity goes beyond Christianity to honor the universal truths in all religions, respecting each individual's right to choose his or her own specific spiritual path.

God is seen as Spirit, the loving source of all that is. God is also "divine energy, continually creating, expressing, and sustaining all creation." Jesus expresses God's divine potential, and certainly not the only one; however, he models to us how we can express our own as well. Unity understands the term "Christ" as pointing to the divinity in all humankind, with Jesus as the great example. However, the invitation is for everyone to realize the same. Each individual is seen as an eternal expression of God with an essential nature that is divine and therefore inherently good. Here, we see the opposite of the Fall/redemption theology, which looks at essential human nature as intrinsically flawed. According to Unity philosophy, similar to the Hindu tradition, the goal of the human is to realize and express his or her divine potential, in the way that not only did Jesus recognize and express his but other master teachers from cultures around the world have done for ages.

The Bible is studied in the context of its cultural development, with the acknowledgment that its various writings reflect the understanding and inspiration of the writers who wrote it, within their own particular framework. It is valued for both its historical and allegorical dimensions, and interpreted metaphysically, that is, from the perspective of humankind's evolutionary journey toward spiritual awakening.[4]

You may learn more at www.unity.org.

Select Bibliography

Abhishiktananda. *Prayer*.

———. *The Secret of Arunachala*.

James Arraj. *Christianity in the Crucible of East-West Dialogue: A Critical Look at Catholic Participation*.

Marcus Borg. *The Heart of Christianity: Rediscovering a Life of Faith*.

———. *The Meaning of Jesus: Two Visions* (written with N. T. Wright).

Shirley du Boulay. *Beyond the Darkness: A Biography of Bede Griffiths*.

———. *The Cave of the Heart: The Life of Swami Abhishiktananda*.

Deepak Chopra. *The Third Jesus: The Christ We Cannot Ignore*.

Matthew Fox. *One River, Many Wells: Wisdom Springing from Global Faiths*.

———. *Sins of the Spirit, Blessings of the Flesh: Lessons for Transforming Evil in Soul and Society*.

Bede Griffiths. *The Cosmic Revelation: A New Way to God*.

———. *Marriage of East and West*.

————. *New Vision of Reality: Western Science, Eastern Mysticism, and Christian Faith.*

————. *Return to the Center.*

————. *River of Compassion: A Christian Commentary on the Bhagavad Gita.*

Thomas Keating. *Invitation to Love: The Way of Christian Contemplation.*

————. *Open Mind, Open Heart: The Contemplative Dimension of the Gospel.*

Jim Marion. *The Death of the Mythic God: The Rise of Evolutionary Spirituality.*

————. *Putting on the Mind of Christ: The Inner World of Christian Spirituality.*

Juan Mascaro. *The Bhagavad Gita.*

————. *The Upanishads.*

Thomas Matus, *Yoga and the Jesus Prayer Tradition: An Experiment in Faith.*

Caroline Myss. *Anatomy of the Spirit: The Seven Stages of Power and Healing.*

Jacob Needleman. *The American Soul: Rediscovering the Wisdom of the Founders.*

————. *Lost Christianity: A Journey of Rediscovery.*

Justin O'Brien. *A Meeting of Mystic Paths: Christianity and Yoga.*

Raimon Panikkar. *Christophany: The Fullness of Man.*

————. *The Experience of God: Icons of the Mystery.*

Ravi Ravindra. *The Yoga of the Christ.*

John Martin Sahajananda. *The Four O'Clock Talks.*

————. *Jesus Christ: A Bridge to Bring Peace to the World.*

————. *Truth Has No Boundaries: Proclaiming the Good News of Peace.*

————. *You Are the Light: Rediscovering the Eastern Jesus.*

Wayne Teasdale. *Bede Griffiths: An Introduction to His Interspiritual Thought.*

————. *A Monk in the World: Cultivating a Spiritual Life.*

————. *The Mystic Heart: Finding a Universal Spirituality in the World's Religions.*

Acknowledgments

I WOULD LIKE TO START BY THANKING MY EDITOR, Jason Gardner, and my publisher, New World Library. They believed in the value of this book and, more important, are committed to promoting a deeper understanding of spirituality to the world. I would simultaneously like to thank the Relaxation Company, a record label that puts out much of my music, which is another important and complementary medium through which I share my energy with the world. I thank Erik Engels, who helped organize and develop this manuscript, and Bonita Hurd for her razor-sharp copyediting. And I thank my wife, spiritual companion, and best friend, Asha, for all her help and support. She sustains the space for me to write, create, travel, and teach. I love you!

I want to thank the Christians I know, people who make me glad of my Christian roots and inspire me to look deeply in appreciation of the tradition I was born into. They include Fr. Gilles Bourdeau, Brother Roph Fernandez, Brother John Martin Sahajananda, and Brother Gregory

Perron, who also helped me research a few areas, as did Fr. Gilles. I thank them for their assistance. Likewise, there are the Hindus I know, who make me grateful for my Hindu connection and ancestry, and they include Swami Swaroopananda and the Sharma family, my spiritual brothers Ajay and Pankaj, their wives and their children, and most assuredly their parents, Raj and Sudesh Sharma.

Last but not least, I thank Claudette Bourdeau Roth, friend and comforter, who has on many occasions during the writing of this work been there for me and supported me, in word and in spirit and in more ways than I can put into words. And I thank you, dear reader, for including this book in your collection. I hope it serves you well and inspires you in your life and your spiritual practice.

Notes

Introduction

1. Matthew Fox, *The A.W.E. Project: Reinventing Education, Reinventing the Human* (Kelowna, BC, Canada: Copperhouse, 2006), 105–6.

2. The guru, in the traditional sense, "is God," and Bede did not function this way. Yet he had many of the qualities exemplified by the term.

3. B. A. Robinson, "Religions of the World," 2007, Religious Tolerance.org, www.religioustolerance.org/worldrel.htm, accessed December 9, 2008.

4. Swami Chidananda, "Yoga and Christianity," Divine Life Society, www.dlshq.org/religions/yogachristian.htm, accessed December 9, 2008. Reproduced from Swami Chidananda's book *Guidelines to Illumination*.

5. From "Indian Bishops Say at Least 60 Killed in Anti-Christian Violence," October 17, 2008, http://afp.google.com/article/ALeqM5hrEca1V4MpK8dwCYBSAiY8jmrIUg, accessed December 16, 2008.

6. "Major Religions of the World Ranked by Number of Adherents," last modified August 9, 2007, www.adherents.com/Religions_By_Adherents.html, accessed December 16, 2008.

Chapter 1

1. From "Politics and Religious Fundamentalism," posted by Arun Gandhi, December 7, 2008, http://newsweek.washington post.com/onfaith/arun_gandhi/2008/12/s_and_religious _fundamentalism.html, accessed December 22, 2008.

2. Modern scholars speculate that, when Jesus used the phrase "turn the other cheek," he could well have been referring to the fact that a Roman soldier would backhand a Jew or slave with his right hand. The backhanded slap was intended as an act of disrespect, so turning the other cheek to such an oppressor would require him to use his palm if he chose to strike again — which would mean altering the status relationship: the slave would now be his equal. In other words, when we present ourselves without fear to an oppressor, we spark some inner light that can trigger his or her return to goodness. Jesus's teachings encourage us to confront evil in this way rather than to recoil in fear or fight back with violence.

3. From Arun Gandhi, email to the author, December 12, 2008.

4. *The World Fact Book* of the Central Intelligence Agency, based on a 2001 consensus and last updated December 4, 2008. From www.cia.gov/library/publications/the-world-factbook/geos/in.html, accessed December 17, 2008.

5. Bede Griffiths, *The Marriage of East and West* (1976; reprint, Tucson: Medio Media, 2003), 12.

6. Today, environmental movements are inspiring a different mentality among Western nations, yet many conservative Christians remain indifferent to ecological concerns. Sadly, many Eastern societies, taking their cue from the West, have yet to embrace environmental standards that will ensure the health of our planet.

7. By this, I mean valuing the symbols and myths of other cultures as valid mediators of the sacred.

8. The Middle Ages had its dark side, too, with both the Crusades and the Spanish Inquisition.

9. Griffiths, *Marriage of East and West*, 4.

10. In recent times, we have discovered that Hindu and Buddhist gurus have not been much different: their actions have been just as abusive and just as scandalous. In chapter 4, I share

some thoughts on how Christianity can contribute to change in the East in this regard.

11. Marcus J. Borg, *The Heart of Christianity: Rediscovering a Life of Faith* (San Francisco: HarperSanFrancisco, 2004), 48–50.

12. By *scientific-minded*, I mean a person who tends to rely on hard, empirical evidence; inferences derived from mathematical calculations; or plausible theoretical speculations based on reputable science data.

13. John Shelby Spong, *A New Christianity for a New World* (San Francisco: HarperSanFrancisco, 2001), 21–22.

14. While such appellations are not without value within certain contexts and communities, they tend to be divisive when relating to other traditions. Moreover, they fail to appeal to the person of science, for the definition of the term has not kept up with the evolution of this aspect of the human mind.

15. The Inner Connection is a Tucson-based organization that hosts superb spiritual conferences.

16. Jim Marion, *Death of the Mythic God: The Rise of Evolutionary Spirituality* (Hampton Roads: Charlottesville, VA, 2004), 70–71.

17. Griffiths, *Marriage of East and West*, 7.

Chapter 2

1. Justin O'Brien, *A Meeting of Mystic Path: Christianity and Yoga* (Saint Paul, MN: Yes International Publishers, 1996), 52–53.

2. Thomas Keating, *Intimacy with God* (New York: Crossroad Publishing, 1996), 46.

3. *Hara* in Zen denotes the physical and spiritual center of the body, which lies one to two inches below the navel, at the base of the abdomen. In Yoga, the equivalent center is the *nabhi*; the term means "center" as well as "navel."

4. *Sunnyata*, in Pali and Sanskrit, means "emptiness" and is often referred to as "the void," an interior space that is simultaneously space, mind, perception, and experience. It is derived from *sunya*, the word for "zero" or "nothing."

5. David Godman, *Living by the Words of Bhagavan* (Tiruvannamalai: Sri Annamali Swami Ashram Trust, 1995), 24–25.

6. Juan Mascaro, *The Upanishads* (New York: Penguin Classics, 1965), 60–61.

7. Dave Shiflett, "Airplane Reading — Inspiration: Your Ultimate Calling," March 2006, www.drwaynedyer.com/articles/wallstreet.php, accessed December 15, 2008. Reprinted from *Wall Street Journal* Online.

8. The quote is from a conversation between Abba Moses and John Cassian. St. John Cassian, *Conferences* (New York: Paulist Press, 1985), 61–63.

9. Ibid.

10. Stephen Mitchell, *The Bhagavad Gita: A New Translation* (New York: Three Rivers Press, 2000), 59–60.

11. There are many "kinds" of Yoga. Although, the word *yoga* means "union," it can also refer to the path or method or means toward that union.

Chapter 3

1. The conclusion of the second point of the Declaration on the Relation of the Church to Non-Christian Religions, *NOSTRA AETATE*, proclaimed by his holiness, Pope Paul VI, on October 28, 1965.

2. Much of the extraordinary artwork at Shantivanam was created by a brilliant artist from England, a man by the name of Jyoti Sahi, who came to live at Shantivanam in the seventies, not long after Bede had taken over the ashram. He and Bede together created this magnificent testimony to the marriage of Hinduism, Yoga, and Christianity.

3. Brother David Steindl Rast, *The Music of Silence* (San Francisco: HarperSanFrancisco, 1995).

4. The opening prefix of the "Om Bhur Bhuvas Svaha" is a formula taken from the Yajurveda; the rest of the mantra, which is the actual Gayatri mantra, occurs in verse 3.62.10 of the Rigveda.

5. This was not the only reason for Bede's inclusion of Sanskrit in the prayers and liturgy. More important, it represented a deep and profound respect for the entire Indian spiritual tradition in our lives.

6. Although "Lokah samastha sukhino bhavanthu" does not

occur in any branch of the Vedas, it is often chanted alongside traditional Vedic prayers. "Asato ma Sadgamaya" is from the Brihadaranyaka Upanishad 1.3.28 and is associated with the White Yajur Veda.

7. This is a famous mantra invocation that opens the Isha Upanishad, associated with the White Yajurveda.

8. This prayer is from the Trisagion (Qadishat Aloho) of the Qawmo.

9. I deal with this extensively in the next chapter.

10. At Shantivanam, we followed the canonical formative process of the Benedictine order (postulant, novice, professed monk), as well as the traditional Yogic system of *sadhaka* (seeker), *brahmacharin* (celibate monk), *sannyasin* (renunciate). These positions sat side by side but each on its own time line. While the canonical process had set periods for each phase, with the decision for progression governed by the abbot, the community, and the religious order, the Yogic system was determined by inner readiness and maturity, determined solely by the teacher, in this case Bede Griffiths.

11. Highly complex ritual sacrifices known as *yajnas* were the main form of worship during the Vedic period (1500 to 500 BCE) and pre-Vedic period, during which offerings were made in a sacrificial fire. It was the demands of these sacrifices that the Yoga tradition and the Buddha reacted against.

12. The *Purusha Sukta* is hymn 10.90 of the Rigveda.

13. John Martin Sahajananda, *Truth Has No Boundaries: Proclaiming the Good News of Peace* (Tiruchirapalli, India: Saccidananda Ashram, n.d.), 68.

Chapter 4

1. Again, I use this term to mean "ego-consciousness." Self-realization — the awakening to Spirit, to enlightenment — is often denoted with a capital *S* (as in *Self-realization*), though this may not be apparent when the word begins a sentence.

2. The Exultet, or Easter Proclamation.

3. Stephen Mitchell, *The Bhagavad Gita: A New Translation* (New York: Three Rivers Press, 2000), 73.

4. Ibid., 193.

5. Ibid., 73.

6. To follow Jesus, then, is to take on this task of repairing the ruptured fabric of life through our own efforts to connect. This is one way of understanding the Christian path as a Yoga.

7. In present-day India, warped notions of sexuality conveyed by movies and television obscure this deep and ancient understanding, and there is a great deal of unhealthy sexual repression. Indians may have to rediscover the spiritual and sacred dimensions of sexuality and its expressions within the culture.

8. This statement by Jesus directly reflects the unified vision of higher consciousness associated with the Ajna (command) chakra, also called the "third eye," which is depicted as a single eye in the center of the forehead. It symbolizes the spiritual eye of unity, in contrast to the eyes of duality that are our physical eyes. Furthermore, this chakra is associated with the pineal gland, which processes light.

9. Sin, in the East, is seen as the result of ignorance, as the lack of awakening to the true Self. In the West, it is seen as the deliberate exercising of free will against goodness and human dignity. There is something in both views that contributes to the "effect" of sin, which is the separation from love.

10. By this I mean the refined and spiritually profound aspects of these approaches.

11. Thomas Keating, *The Invitation to Love: The Way of Christian Contemplation* (New York: Continuum, 2001), 58.

12. While the choice may be made outside of time, the effects of this choice are time bound. For this reason, it's necessary to continually choose to sustain movement in any direction, either for or against the cause of love.

13. Keating, *The Invitation to Love*, 9.

Chapter 5

1. Matthew Fox, *Meditations with Meister Eckhart* (Santa Fe, NM: Bear and Company, 1983), 15.

2. As I explain later, I believe that the ego always remains. It is the level of transparency and pliability that changes, and this condition is to be nurtured and maintained throughout one's existence in the body.

3. Thomas Keating, *Open Mind, Open Heart: The Contemplative Dimension of the Gospel* (New York: Continuum, 2006), 71.

4. Yet, as I just mentioned, Bede did have an ego. The difference is that an enlightened ego does not harm others or oneself.

5. Graham V. Ledgerwood, "Dark Night of the Soul," 2001, The Mystic.org, www.themystic.org/dark-night/index.htm, accessed December 10, 2008.

6. From the editor's preface to "The Practice of the Presence of God," 1999. The entire text of this work can be read at www.PracticeGodsPresence.com. All passages quoted in this chapter, including selections from the editor's preface, are from this gracious online source available to anyone and everyone. Go read it.

7. Keating, *Open Mind, Open Heart*, 71.

Chapter 6

1. Later, Christianity came to regard Christ as the fulfillment of all the other traditions, and today it perhaps sees Christ as the "first among equals." However, Christianity, to its credit, is in constant evolution.

2. Jacob Needleman, *The American Soul: Rediscovering the Wisdom of the Founders* (New York: Jeremy P. Tarcher/Putnam, 2002), 16.

3. Hindus and Yogis often state that divine bliss is equivalent to the love that dominates Christianity. While one may argue that the outpouring of love found at the heart of the Holy Trinity could be the same as the divine bliss experienced by the Yogi and Indian mystic, the difference is that the love component in the Christian approach does not require Yogic effort or absorption in ultimate reality (Samadhi) in order to be experienced. In fact, this love, as expressed in Christianity, is an experience of ultimate reality that one can encounter even in states of separation, in states of sin, and despite accumulated karma. The most powerful mystical experience for the Christian is this fundamental love; it combines with the implicit faith that this love is always available to the entire person despite all of his or her limitations.

4. Caroline Myss, *Invisible Acts of Power: Personal Choices That Create Miracles* (New York: Free Press, 2004), 16.

5. It is unfortunate that Christianity denies the validity of this experience for anyone other than Jesus. Yet this experience has been central to Indian spirituality for thousands of years. Also unfortunate is the fact that popular Christianity does not encourage its practitioners to seek deeper levels of mystical experience. These circumstances further underline the benefit of blending the emphases of the two traditions.

6. Readers unfamiliar with Yoga should understand that there is a strong moral component at its foundation.

7. Bede Griffiths, *Return to the Center* (Springfield, IL: Templegate, 1977), 11.

8. Stephen Mitchell, *The Bhagavad Gita: A New Translation* (New York: Three Rivers Press, 2000), 59–60.

9. *Original blessing* is a term coined by the Reverend Matthew Fox, who wrote a book by that title challenging Western Christian theology to rethink its foundational model.

10. Cynthia Bourgeault, *The Wisdom Jesus: Transforming Heart and Mind — A New Perspective on Christ and His Message* (Boston & London: Shambhala, 2008), 37.

11. Bede Griffiths, *The Marriage of East and West* (1976; reprint, Tucson: Medio Media, 2003), 116.

12. Sri Aurobindo, *The Life Divine* (Twin Lakes, WI: Lotus Press, first ed. 1985).

13. There are likely others I have failed to mention, and still others I have not heard of. If so, these omissions are not deliberate, and I welcome information about interspiritual individuals, websites, books, DVDs, and audio CDs.

Epilogue

1. John Martin Sahajananda, *Mission without Conversion: O Lord, Make Us Instruments of Peace — An Open Letter to Christians* (Saccidananda Ashram, India).

2. David Boren, *A Letter to America* (Norman: University of Oklahoma Press, 2008).

3. Not to be confused with Brahmin, which is the Hindu priest and the caste to which he belongs, or Brahma, who is the

Creator God or creative force in the universe. Brahman is the
Great Mystery, Ultimate Reality, the Alpha and the Omega,
the Absolute Godhead, the Supreme Spirit.

Interspiritual Practices, Resources, and Select Bibliography

1. "Paraclete," Wikipedia.org, http://en.wikipedia.org/wiki/
   Paraclete, accessed December 10, 2008.
2. From "The Life of Bahá'u'lláh," www.bahai.org; "The Bahá'í
   Faith," www.austinbahai.org./?view=intro; and "Basic Teachings of Bahá'u'lláh," www.austinbahai.org./?view=basic, all
   accessed December 17, 2008.
3. From "Principles of Creation Spirituality," www.creation
   spirituality.info/Principles.html, accessed December 17, 2008.
   The webpage states that the list is taken from the book
   Confessions: The Making of a Post-Denominational Priest by
   Matthew Fox.
4. Condensed from "Unity: A Path for Spiritual Living,"
   www.unity.org/index.php?src=gendocs&ref=IdentityStatement
   &category=About%20Us, accessed December 17, 2008.

About the Author

RUSSILL PAUL IS A WORLD-RENOWNED MUSICIAN, blending Indian and contemporary music in his recordings and performances, as well as a teacher of Eastern spirituality. He trained simultaneously as a monk and a Yogi under the direction of the renowned sage and mystic Bede Griffiths in South India for close to five years and has taught in graduate and postgraduate spirituality programs for the past seventeen years. Russill presently offers personal spirituality training through his Yogic Mystery School, a distance-learning spirituality program that combines multimedia learning with online support. He also offers an annual pilgrimage and retreat and other special programs in India in addition to presenting workshops and retreats across the United States and Canada.

For more information, please visit www.russillpaul.com. For news, study groups, and updates about this book, click on "Jesus in the Lotus."